Praise for Dr. Ed Iannuccilli

"Dr. Ed Iannuccilli is a Rhode Island treasure. His poignant reminiscing on life growing up in Providence, from the sights and sounds and smells of the neighborhood, to family life and the local businesses to which so many can remember and relate, are a joy to read, and we have been fortunate to share on GoLocalProv.com. To have them now featured in one place – and in one book – will be a real gift to readers."

– *Kate Nagle, GoLocalProv News Editor*

"Ed is the ultimate storyteller. He takes you back in time. With his writing, you can taste the sauce at the Sunday dinner, feel the seat in the old movie theater, and taste the ice cream on that hot summer day in the city. He is a remarkable guide in traveling through time."

– *Josh Fenton, CEO and Co-founder of GoLocal 24*

"Dr. Ed Iannuccilli uses his capacious memory, empathy, unpretentious, yet elegant, style, and close observation of the passing scene to create vivid word pictures from the past and today. His essays remind us of the treasures we can enjoy in everyday life if we but stop, look, listen, and remember. He brings us memorable sights, sounds, and smells (particularly of Italian cooking!) And along the way, he serves us as a superb informal social historian."

– *Robert Whitcomb, GoLocal24 columnist, Editor of New England Diary, author, editor, and former Senior Editor at the International Herald Tribune and the Providence Journal*

"Here are great selections from Dr. Ed Iannuccilli's writing: kind, wise, warm, and true. Dr. Iannuccilli makes the regular things in life, its textures, smells, and tastes, sparkle in the special light of memory. A great book to come home to."

– *Michael Fine, M.D., Author of Rhode Island Stories*

ALSO BY ED IANNUCCILLI

My Story Continues: Fron Neighborhood to Junior High School

Growing Up Italian: Grandfather's Fig Tree and Other Stories

Whatever Happened to Sunday Dinner?

Growing Up Italian: Collected Stories (e-book)

A Whole Bunch
of
500-Word Stories

ED IANNUCCILLI

A Whole Bunch of 500-Word Stories
Copyright © 2022 Ed Iannuccilli
All Rights Reserved

No part of this book may be used or reproduced in any manner whatsoever without the written permission of the author, except in the case of brief quotations. For information, contact:

Edward A. Iannuccilli, 70 High Street, Bristol, RI 02809-2011
401.787.0814 • edwritesri@gmail.com

Designed by Randy Walters
randywalters.com

Set in Garamond Classico

First Edition
Printed in the United States of America
ISBN: 978-0-578-38621-8

Dedication

to Bob Whitcomb
who got me started

and Josh Fenton
who kept me going

and thank you to GoLocalProv
for hosting my stories
and endorsing their publication

CONTENTS

Introduction 1

Chapter I – Growing Up 3
Overnight in a Tent. Well, Maybe. 3
My First Time at the Racetrack 5
Gum Chewing 6
The Heat of a Childhood Summer 8
Marshmallows and Potatoes for Roasting 9
Crabbin' on a Summer Evening 11
Boom Box and Fats Domino 12
I Hear the Crack of the Bat 14
We Feared Polio and Ringworm 15
Would I Get This Close Today? 17
Summer Movies and Citronella 18
A Carnival. It Must Be Summer 20
A Summer Love 22
Summer Sunday Morning 23
Eddie Zack and Campbell's Soup 25
The Funnies 26
My First Job: Paperboy 28
My Paper Route on Health Avenue 29
The Folks on My Paper Route 31

Chapter II – Neighborhood 33
A Snow Man and a Snow Fort 33
Bullied, I Guess 35
Wireless in Rhode Island 36

Life Lessons from a Pinball Machine *38*
Trolleys on the Avenue *39*
Do You Come to Providence? *41*
Bring Back the Peddler *42*
I Was Always a Hobo *44*
The Bell of the Ice Cream Truck *45*

CHAPTER III – PARENTS *48*
What Do You Keep of Your Parents' Belongings? *48*
What's Your Favorite Number? *50*
Dad Handles the Asbestos *51*
Mom and Dad Loved Coffee *53*
Who Purged My Comic Books? *55*

CHAPTER IV – GRANDPARENTS. IMMIGRATION *57*
Why Did They Settle in Rhode Island? *57*
My Grandfather's Diaries *59*
A Grandfather's Courage *60*
Why Didn't They Smile *62*
They Had Their Sayings *63*

CHAPTER V – HOLIDAYS *66*
Magical Memories of the Holiday Season *66*
Doings on the 4th *68*
My Italo-Turkey Day *69*
Downtown with Mom at Christmas *71*
Dad's Christmas Tree *72*
Blindsided at Thanksgiving *74*

CHAPTER VI – TIME *76*
How Old Do You Feel? *76*
Trying to Understand Time *78*
Time on Ellis Island *79*
Can I Go Backward in Time? *81*
Even the Garden Has Its Time *82*
Time on My Wrist *84*
Are Friendships Governed by the Passage of Time? *85*
The Days Get Longer by a Minute *87*

CHAPTER VII – FOOD *89*
Of Tortillas and Omelets to Die For *89*
Eels Are Not My Favorite *91*
Eat Your Lentils *92*
Time for Hot Chocolate *94*
Plants Taste Like Beef. So What? *95*
What's Not to Like About Roasted Chestnuts *97*
Learning to Cook. Starting a Business, and Giving Back *98*
What Is Your Favorite Pie? *100*
Shifting Blame in the Middle of Chaos *101*
Hope and Main Does It. Again *103*
The Mt. Hope Farm Contributes *104*

CHAPTER VIII – HUMOR *107*
A Surprise in the Bowling Alley *107*
The Old Guy Is in Good Shape *109*
A Surprise in the Doctor's Office *110*
The Day Started Well *112*

Will I Ever Be Able to Whistle? *113*
How to Sell Your Home *115*
Do You Know What Druthers Are? *116*
My Brief Time on a Pony *118*
Why Wear a Necktie? *119*
The Coat Wore Me Down *121*
Can We All Be Shmoos? *122*

CHAPTER IX – HEALTH CARE *125*
A Leap for Alzheimer's *125*
Whither Hiccupping? *127*
A Siren Call to Quarantine *128*
Diary of a Writer in Quarantine *130*
Health Care Workers *131*

CHAPTER X – TRAVEL *133*
My First Night in Italy *133*
The Splendor of the Kentucky Derby *135*

CHAPTER XI – NATURE *137*
Of Peepers and Mayflies *137*
The Pleasure of Hippocrates' Tree *139*
The Excitement of a Storm *xx140*
What's Not to Like About a Snowstorm? *142*

CHAPTER XII – WRITING *144*
A Door Opens *144*
I Dangle a Participle *146*

Take Time to Write *147*
Learning is a Delicacy *149*
Write Your Tale *150*
Purging Books *152*

Chapter XIII – Ramblings *154*
The Fashion of Wearing a Vest *154*
In This Confinement, What Do I Miss Most? *156*
Lessons from the Hawk and the Dove *157*
Once Masks Were Fun *159*
A Man Who is Making a Difference *160*
Does Zoom Work for Me? *162*
What Color is Your Parachute *163*
I Flunk the Draft Test *165*

About the Author *169*

INTRODUCTION

Why a bunch of 500-word stories?
When I was hired to write for GoLocal, it was suggested that I limit each weekly piece to 500 words. Sometimes limited words are tougher than freewheeling essays, so I had to give it some thought. Once I got into the rhythm, it came much more easily, as did the topics.

When people ask how I have so much to write about, my reply is that they need to look and listen as there is a story at every corner, in every conversation, in memories.

So, thank you for reading these essays. They are fun. I promise more.

CHAPTER I

GROWING UP

Overnight in a Tent. Well, Maybe

I was a kid who never wanted to leave home in the summer, or anytime, so I was never "sentenced" to a camp. My mom knew I could never survive in the wild jungle. I liked being around the home or at a beach cottage where, on my own or with trusted friends, I could wander freely in the dappled light of the oak trees, listen to cicadas, play stickball or gawk at caterpillars and turtles at the nearby stream.

That was enough adventure for me. I never got a badge or roamed the night forest.

At eight, I was lucky to have Wally as a friend. He lived on the first floor of a two-family house across the street. Four years older, he was professorial, with mountains of knowledge about to explode from his wide-eyed, smiling face. While I boasted of going downtown with my mother to see a movie, Wally told captivating stories of Boy Scout Camp adventures. I was not at all envious.

Wally slept in a tent pitched every summer in his backyard. One afternoon, he asked me to join him and Andy, another Scout, to an overnight. "Yes," I said, with enthusiasm. Wow, a night in the wild with the big guys. Wally's mother reassured my mom that she would "Keep an eye on things." Confident, I saw no need for her to monitor me.

At sunset, I shuffled across the street in my pajamas and slippers. Wally and Andy shared camp stories, tales of nights, and creatures that roamed the woods. Wally pointed out the North Star. I told him I saw it, but I think it was a streetlight. In the distance were the sandbanks, barely visible in the fading light.

Wally's Mom shut her kitchen light. The guys fell asleep. I tossed, sat up, looked for the North Star and listened … groans, snaps, howls, barks, mews, and steps … a garage door closing, an engine purring, a television, a cough, a ball game – the Boston Braves? Lights flickered. The cellar light was on in the house next door. Was something moving? I never realized how long it took for the moon to move. I thought of my bed, my room. I shook Wally. "Eddie. Whatsup?"

"I wanna go home."

Wally's Mom appeared from the shadows. "Come along." I rolled my pillow and blanket into a ball, tightened my pajama string, and put on my slippers. We crossed the street. Wally's Mom left me with Mom at the door. "Thank you."

In the comfort of my bedroom, I slid under fresh, cool sheets oozing the smell of soap. I turned on my radio. "Who knows what evil lurks in the hearts of men? The Shadow knows." I snuggled my head into the fluffy pillow and pulled the sheets up under my chin. The moonlight rolled softly over my blanket. Ted Williams's picture stood tall on the dresser.

I looked at the clock. 9:15. Hmm, earlier than I thought.

What a great adventure.

My First Time at the Racetrack

I have the good fortune to be a trustee of the R.I. Historical Society and a member of the committee planning their upcoming spring event, Horsing Around: Rhode Island's Horse Racing Heyday. The Historical Society recently obtained thousands of negatives of photographs taken at Narragansett Racetrack, which opened in 1934 and closed in 1978.

I was a student at Providence College when a gang of us decided to go to Narragansett to see the races. Until then, I had only two 'peripheral' exposures to horse racing: I worked as a driver for my uncle's market when, on occasion, he asked me to go to the corner newspaper store to get him the daily racing form which I believed he called *The Armstrong*. The other was a carnival game where to win, we had to get the mechanical horses to race up a slanted board to the top.

The first thing that surprised me when I walked up the ramp to the Narragansett Track was its size. Though it was late in the lifetime of the raceway, it had the capacity for 40,000 people. In its heyday, the track consisted of a one-mile racing oval, a huge grandstand, a row of betting and paying booths, a clubhouse, and lots of barns.

According to the Historical Society, by the late 1930s, "Gansett," as it was popularly known, was the most profitable track in the country, attracting crowds of 40,000 or more. In the late '30s and '40s, it became a gathering place for celebrities such as Milton Berle, Cab Calloway, Bing Crosby, Babe Ruth, Jack Dempsey, and Lou Gehrig. Impressive place.

I stood for a moment at the top of the ramp to admire the track and to watch a race. The bell rang and as the horses bolted out of the gate to the eruption of "They're off," a murmur arose in escalating decibels. As the horses rounded the near turn, I was astounded by the swell of emotion, cheering, yelling, screaming; a passion I did not understand. "What the heck is this?" I wondered. "Why is the noise rising to this pitch?"

It drifted to a muffled murmur as human feet shuffled in place or clicked along to the pay booths. I turned to the usher, "How do you bet on a race?"

"OK, son, here's my advice. Ya see that exit. Go to and through it, don't turn roun 'n nevah come back."

"Aw, you gotta be kidding." Forsaking his advice, I went to place a bet, not sure on what horse or with what reasoning. I returned to the stands. "They're off!"

As they made the far turn, I stood on my toes and stretched my neck, now realizing why people roared. It was about money. Holding ticket on high, now I began to roar, jump, and stomp. I wanted to win. "Go four! Go!"

By the time they hit the finish line, I was sweating from jumping and hoarse from screaming.

I tore my ticket and went for another.

Gum Chewing

Last weekend, I was watching The US Open Golf Championship and noticed something I had not seen before. Some of the golfers were chewing gum, to relax or help them to concentrate. I'm not sure. It reminded me of my gum-chewing days.

I published a story some years ago about going to the movies on my first date. At one point, just after I put my arm around her shoulder, I squirmed and reached under the seat with my free hand. There I found a minefield of immovable, petrified gum that seemed like a map of the world in relief. "Eeow. Just during my most romantic moment." I quickly removed my hand – from the seat, that is.

I chewed lots of gum. Why not? The baseball players did. One player, Nellie Fox, a little second baseman for the White Sox had a giant wad of tobacco wrapped in chewing gum ballooning his cheek. He seemed fine though he spit rivers of brown juice.

Most of the time, I chomped on Fleer's Dubble Bubble, a favorite because it came with cards of baseball players. The cards lasted, but the gum wore out quickly, taking on the consistency of tar and the flavor of sawdust within minutes. I switched to Wrigley's Spearmint because Mom and my aunts chewed it as a breath freshener and a (doubtful) teeth cleaner. It was awful, medicinal-like.

I tried Juicy Fruit, sweeter, but it also lost its flavor quickly. I recall the song, "Does Your Chewing Gum Lose Its Flavor on the Bedpost Overnight?" Mine did long before it hit the post. So back to the pinks of bubble gum; Fleer's Dubble Bubble is my favorite, though Bazooka, wrapped with a Bazooka Joe comic strip, was a close second.

Not only was the bubble gum flavor superior, but it was also designed for blowing bubbles. There was a certain way I used my tongue to flatten the gum in a circle against the back of my teeth and blow. Some bubbles I blew were bigger than my head. Sure enough, you guessed it. The big kids popped it, and it stuck on my face and in my hair. Mom trundled after me with her scissors, cutting out a chunk of sticky, rubbery hair, the bald patch now a humiliating symbol of my bubble-blowing proficiency.

Bubble gum came with those tall-tale, illogical, frightening parent wives' tales: "If you swallow it, it will collect and make a huge ball that will block your intestines. It sticks to your stomach for seven years." As a gastroenterologist, I assure you that it is most unlikely that swallowed gum will not be digested.

Over the years, I tried Chicklets and Tutti Frutti but, though they were cute, they could never match the pink pleasure of the 'wad.' Today, the gum is sold in a variety of shapes and flavors like blueberry pie and tomato soup (so they say). Why would they do that to gum?

I'm wondering if I might try chewing gum tomorrow during my golf round.

The Heat of a Childhood Summer

When the heat of summer is upon us, I hear a common refrain: "When I was a kid it was always like this. We had no air conditioning. If we had a fan, it was one of those desk ones with no cage. It circulated stifling air." Well, they're not far off. When I was growing up in a third-floor tenement in Providence, the days were hot, the nights were brutal.

The old saying was "Summer days were hot enough to fry an egg on the sidewalk." I'm sure we tried that once or twice. We cooled under sprinklers or swam at the Olneyville Boys Club, sometimes at the Narragansett shore. We made tarballs from hot tar scraped off the steaming streets. Sewing bees sewed in the daytime, cicadas hummed at night and lightning bugs sparkled on their evening soirees. We did not have a thermometer to measure the heat in our tenement but, if we had, I'm sure it would hit ninety plus. And that was day after day after day.

Nights in the clammy oven of our third-floor bedroom could be unbearable. The air was still and silent. Adjacent homes were close, and the rare breeze that trickled through was a welcomed friend. Time passed slowly. I tossed. I turned. I walked around the house. Sweat trickled under my arms. The occasional mosquito that got through the screen was an annoying pest that was never satisfied. To sleep was not difficult; it was impossible. Nevertheless, those nights lent themselves to comforting memories – in retrospect.

The heat drove the adults outside. Hearing soft chatter from the first-floor porch below, my brother Peter and I decided to follow the murmurs, muffled laughter, the calls of the cicadas, the chirps of the crickets, and the lively display of firefly illuminations. The street dogs were resting.

Attracted by the sounds below as bees to honey, we rolled out of bed and snuck down the stairs to sit shirtless on the porch floor off to the side, hopefully unnoticed. Mom, Aunt Della, and Grandma glanced and continued talking. As I remember, Mom was in her pajamas, Aunt Della in a nightgown, and Grandma in a housedress and backless black slippers.

The moonlight and layers of stars sprinkled the clear night. More glows came from nearby streetlights. Bugs flickered to tap the lights' metal hats. Shadows from the trees and houses painted the street. Mumbling came from neighbors sitting nearby. They too were attempting to chat away the heat. The sounds were comforting as people made the best of the hotness. They were used to much tougher situations.

Peter and I sat motionless, moving only to smush a mosquito. We sat on that porch for what seemed like hours late into the night. "Time for bed, kids." Up we trundled.

I listened to the murmurs below while waiting for a breeze, any breeze. Finally, we dozed to the ongoing music of the voices.

Why did it seem so much hotter in those days? How did we survive it? Easy. We had a porch.

Marshmallows and Potatoes for Roasting

I'm not sure why I thought of marshmallows and baked potatoes today. It was because the summer heat reminded me of roasting something by a campfire.

I loved summer. Its sweet smells: a newly cut lawn, dirt of the garden, a fresh tomato, the sweat of a game, the cool of the sprinkler, and steam from the rain seemed to be a part of every day. When it rained, the splattering drops intensified the reflection of the sun that bounced off the street. It yielded a smell as fresh as a peach and as stale as a musty cellar. I learned later in science class that the smell was ozone, oxygen with an extra molecule.

We played games in the nearby hills, believing we were anything from Army guys to men of the frontier. It depended on what movie we saw that week.

In those hills, we built a fire pit for baking potatoes by digging a hole deep into the cool sand, surrounding it with rocks, adding gathered tinder, and burying the potatoes in it. The potatoes took way longer than expected, but were worth the effort when we dug them out and put them aside to cool while we played.

A potato cooked in a campfire somehow tastes noticeably different (and better) than one cooked any other way. Burned on the outside, it was soft and delicious on the inside. The partially burned skin also was good, combining a charcoal taste with a pleasing crunch. It was just because we cooked it ourselves in survival exercise. Or maybe because we were kids, we didn't know what we were eating. I guess if Mom served it, I wouldn't eat it.

And then there were marshmallows on the beach as in, "Let's roast marshmallows." Anytime anyone lit a fire, someone screamed it with passion, as if the marshmallows were something to worship. On a cool night at the beach, with waves crashing, the moon shining, the stars glittering, the heat of the fire, and a cool breeze foiling the mosquitoes, it was.

Made from the sap of the mallow plant, whipped egg whites, water, and sugar syrup, each marshmallow was a domed square perfectly formed for roasting on a stick. They melted quickly. A skilled marshmallow expert could crisp it just enough, twirl the stick to catch the flow, bring it to the lips, blow and steer the dripping delight into the hungry mouth where, with a simple squish, it floated down and away. Marshmallows had an indefinable, addictive flavor that made you think you could eat the whole package, but after just two (maybe three), the yearning quickly diminished. If you weren't careful, you could go marshmallow mad and eat too many. That's when I grew to dislike them.

Over the years, there were the marshmallow recipes that tried to win me back; the fluffernutter and some sort of square mix with Rice Krispies. Neither did it for me.

I'll just sit by that cozy fire while you all roast.

Crabbin' on a Summer Evening

I stared at the blue clouds dangling as if tethered on fishing lines. The beach glistened as the light of the setting sun gave way to an early moon. My sunburned skin was tight and tender, and the salted hair on my arms bristled under the rub of my sweatshirt. The heat of a beach day turned to a cooler evening. Carrying pails, off we trekked to the far end to catch crabs.

I looked over my shoulder at the variety store's red shingled roof growing smaller as we walked further. Late day beachers were sitting on folding chairs, books in their laps, eyes fixed on the horizon, riveted by the rhythm of the waves.

I swung my red pail with the white handle and leaned forward into the gentle evening wind, a wind that at other times took my kite to those same rocks. The soft sand yielded to mud; the mud gave way to sudsy water.

Beyond the rocks was a mansion on a bluff. I loved that house; a sprawling single-story, yellow home with a black-shingled roof and white gutters. A path wound its way from that house to the rocks. I wondered if rich people crabbed.

Rocks of all sizes in shades of black, gray, green, and brown were strewn with seaweed, moss, fishhooks, and a network of frayed fishing lines. Periwinkles were perched like rows of dunce caps.

For bait, I pulled a large, tenacious mussel from its bed, smashed it with a rock, and tied a string around it. I threw seaweed into the pail, dipped my mussel into the water, and waited. The first crab inched out from under the rock. Back he went. Patience. Dangle the bait. Out and back, he went. Out again, he paused, grabbed the mussel with his claws, and dipped his head into the flesh. I pulled slowly. He was on. I jiggled the crab over the pail, and he fell.

Bunches more came. I loaded the pail and watched them crawl, one over the other, along the smooth sides, undaunted, no matter how many times they slipped back. Like the sunset, it was time to go.

We slipped over the rocks to the shore, the store in the distance. I turned. The rocks diminished under a thin veil of dusk. The waves washed my footsteps away.

I showed the catch to Dad. "What are you going to do with them?"

"Keep 'em."

"And then what?"

"Don't know. Just have them, I guess."

"They'll die, you know. They need to be in the water. It might not be a bad idea to let them go." We walked to the water's edge. I inverted the pail and dumped the crabs. With claws held high, they scurried into the sea, waving, hopefully finding their way back to the rocks.

I coddled pieces of smooth beach glass in my pocket. A soft breeze carried the whiff of seaweed. It was time for a frozen Charleston Chew.

Boom Box and Fats Domino

The other day, as I was driving, Diane and I noticed a nearby church festival and a nicely attired band about to play. Loving band music, I slowed down and asked Diane to lower her window so we could listen as we drove by. Just as she did, a young man sped by in the inner lane.

Baseball cap backward, he had his windows open and his radio booming a loud, rhythmic beat. Predominated by a bass drum, the biggest one ever recorded, and not the one in the parade, it shook the street and rattled our innards. It 'hands-down' would have drowned the drumbeat of the awaiting band.

The driver was rockin', lovin' his music, bopping his head, and rhythmically rotating his shoulders. He was into it and wanted us to appreciate the music and his taste. The beginning band music by the church vaporized in the tumult of his broadcast. "That's annoying and aggravating," I blurted.

"Why, didn't you do that when you were a teenager?" I loved

Diane's gently pointed rhetorical question, which meant "C'mon, I did that when I was a kid, and so did you."

Smiling, I replied, "Yes, I sure did."

"To what songs did you bare open your soul and your car windows?"

"Why, Marty Robbins' "A White Sport Coat and a Pink Carnation" and "Earth Angel" by The Penguins. And, oh yes – there was "I'm Walkin'" by Fats Domino." The Fat Man could rattle the car while I kept the beat, knocking the heel of my hand on the steering wheel.

I remember taking a walk on our quiet Bristol street early one Sunday morning. In the distance and out of view, I heard the detonations from a car radio. As the driver turned the corner, my mustard flared, and I (stupidly) strolled to the center of the street to stop the young man. "Yes, Sir."

"Do you have any idea how loud that is? Do you know there are nurses who worked all night saving lives and are trying to sleep?" (A little fib to make a point).

"I'm sorry, Sir (that Sir thing again). They're not even the best speakers, ya know."

"OK. Keep it down if you can." Off he went.

Summer meant windows down and radio dials up. It was even better when you had a date sitting close, enjoying the music, enjoying each other.

Sure, I was an offender those many years ago, but I used nothing more than the installed, non-supplemented speakers of my Dad's Pontiac's radio. I doubt the sonic waves traveled more than to the curbside.

Today, the speakers are too big, the bass too high. As I get older, the levels of noise can be extreme. Nonetheless, I realize that what we all did may have been a distraction, if not to those on the sidewalk, more likely to me as I pushed buttons to find my favorite songs.

Who could deny being entertained by Fats Domino when I drove by?

I Hear the Crack of the Bat

My brother, an inveterate baseball fan, spends his winters in Florida. When I spoke with him last week, I asked if he would get to Ft. Myers to see his (our) beloved Red Sox. "I'm going today. I'll be looking for a sausage sandwich." He had Fenway in mind.

And so, in late winter, though March Madness has not yet started, the Celtics and Bruins are still playing, and the Boston Marathon is a bit in the distance, thoughts of baseball creep into my head. Spring is closer today because of our mild winter. I have seen the early blooms of crocuses. I am anticipating more buds and the pop of blossoms.

In the springs of my youth, the baseball mitts and bats stored in the cellar were awakenings like sleeping bears, frogs, and baby chicks. Away went the heavy coats, hats, scarves, and gloves. We spent more time outside, taped old balls, rubbed new ones, neatsfoot oiled our gloves. We played catch and took some batting practice, toting an old bat with a nail driven into the sweet spot.

Not all baseball springs are easy. When my children were playing, my Dad and I watched many a game in frigid temperatures. Wearing winter coats and heavy gloves, we often hustled back to the car to turn on the engine and warm. The cold aluminum stands had the same physical properties as the new aluminum bats; one stung hand, the other bums.

The knock of the wooden bat was now the ring of metal, and a high-pitched ping feeling bad for the players and a little guilty (not much) for warming ourselves, we eventually returned to sit on those cold stands or stand behind the home plate fence. The first baseman was wearing a hooded sweatshirt under his uniform. The second baseman wore a toque and a windbreaker. The guy at third had a heavy sweater. The batters swung as if they needed grease. The pitcher blew into his hand. The outfielders were jumping up and down. The coaches wore mittens and clapped a lot. "Hurry up, kid! Throw the ball," barked the umpire. "We gotta get outta here. Strike! Close enough."

So, what if we sat on cold bleachers, swung our arms to keep warm, or ran back to the car. No matter. Dad and I were back on a ballfield watching the kids in the spring of our lives. Together.

Baseball wakes everything in nature ... trees, grasses, flowers, animals, players, fans ... from the long sleep of winter. Here are the last two stanzas of the Milton Bracker poem, "Tomorrow!"

> *And tossing the ball out*
> *And yelling Play Ball!*
> *(Who cares about fall-out –*
> *At least, until fall?)*
>
> *Let nothing sour*
> *This sweetest hour.*
> *The baseball season's*
> *Back in flower!*

Get out those gloves and bats! Play ball! The rite of spring means allegiance to the game.

We Feared Polio and Ringworm

As I've read and listened to the hundreds of stories about the coronavirus, I am reminded of the days of my youth when we feared the sword of two infections: polio and ringworm. Yes, the sword because at any moment, the mythical sword of Damocles (of whom I learned in high school) might fall.

The story dates to an ancient parable popularized by Cicero, whose version centers on the unhappy, powerful, tyrannical king, Dionysius II, who once ruled over Syracuse in Sicily during the fourth and fifth centuries BC. Because his iron-fisted rule made him many enemies, he was tormented by fears of assassination.

A court sycophant, Damocles, showered him with compliments and remarked how blissful his life must be. Dionysius replied, "Do you wish to taste my good fortune?" When Damocles agreed, the king seated him on a golden couch and ordered servants to wait on him. Just as Damocles was starting to enjoy his life, he noticed that the king had hung a razor-sharp sword from the ceiling, positioned over Damocles' head, suspended only by a single strand of horsehair. From then on, the courtier's fear made it impossible for him to savor the opulence of his life.

It was a blinding, bright day in the summer of my youth. Steamy waves of heat seeped from the street, the rubber of my sneaker soles was hot, and a rim of sweat mustached my lip. A black ambulance passed by and absorbed some of that brightness. It crawled; somber. A person in white sat next to a small person lying on a stretcher. The ambulance was transporting a kid with polio to the Chapin Hospital in Providence.

I feared polio and the iron lung, but the problem seemed remote. I feared ringworm even more. "Why is that kid wearing a stocking on his head?"

"He has ringworm. Some bug rots yer hair, and it begins ta fall out and rings form on ya scalp. They shave yer hair, slap gooey medicine on, and wrap it with mesh or a stocking.

Hor-ra-bul."

"How do you get it?"

"From restin' yer head on the seat in the movies." So, that summer, there was no pool, no carnival, and no movies.

I came home one day and turned on the television to hear that Dr. Salk had discovered a vaccine to prevent polio. We stood in line for hours to get the 'shot.' As I walked away holding my arm, I looked back at the windows of the Chapin Hospital and thought of the kids inside for whom the shot came too late; in an iron lung, unable to run, swim or breathe on their own.

The parable of Damocles became a common motif in medieval literature, and the phrase "Sword of Damocles" is used as a term to describe looming danger. Hanging by a thread has become shorthand for a fraught or precarious situation.

We kids feared the thread would be cut by the threat of polio, or ringworm.

And now, the coronavirus.

Would I Get This Close Today?

When I was a kid, I never thought being too close to someone might cause a problem. As I contemplate today's confinement issue, I am reminded of two happenings.

My Dad's self-proclaimed uncle, Africa, was a distant cousin. I encountered him when he visited my aunts on an occasional Sunday. He wore a tattered, black overcoat that dropped to the top of his muddy, wrinkled black boots. He waddled like a duck, the toes of his boots spread wide, his lower legs flailing in rhythm, his wrinkled hands nearly touching the ground. When he sat, the coat touched the floor.

"I gave him that coat years ago," said Dad.

He beckoned me with a crooked finger. "Viene qua." As I approached, he burbled, "You know me? Eh? You like-a me?'

"Yes. You're Uncle Africa. Yes, I like you."

He smiled with damaged, tobacco-stained teeth through an uncombed, uncut mustache. I arched away, my feet in place. He reached into his vest pocket with two fingers and pulled out a silver dollar, a coin so big and shiny that I could not resist; smell, shaggy or not, I plucked it from his fingers, turned, and bolted.

As years passed, I've thought of Uncle Africa and his immigrant spirit, sad that I did not know more about him. Who was he? Where was his family? Where was his home in Italy? What did he do there? Why did he come here? Why a silver dollar?

Uncle Africa is long gone, and so are my silver dollars.

And then there was my grandmother's eccentric friend, Francesco (Frangeesk). He wore a dark blue, three-piece pinstriped suit with high, black, weathered boots laced to the top. His shirt collar was a sweaty yellow. His beady eyes centered on a wrinkled face fronted by a beaked nose. His laugh spilled from his sawed-off, crooked yellow teeth. His garbled dialect was coated with the smell of wine. Most of the time, I succeeded in avoiding him, but he tickled my curiosity one day.

His walk to visit grandmother started with a stop at a local bar. His entertainment started when he beckoned me. Curious, I inched closer. As I approached, he opened his jacket. In the right-side vest pocket, he carried a watch and an attractive pearl-handled knife attached to a chain attached to a vest button. He was holding a tiny sparrow. It moved.

He released the bird. Startled, I jumped back, not realizing that the bird's foot was tied to a string which was also tied to a button on his vest. The bird flew straight up only to hit the end of the tethered string, "boink," and snap back, "twang," flapping his wings, going nowhere. However, the bird was luckier than I; he flew through an open window when released. Though frightened, I was comforted.

I never knew what getting too close might bring. But today, I do, and we should.

Unlike that little kid, we have been warned.

Summer Movies and Citronella

In the '50s, my family rented a cottage at the Narragansett shore. We kids went to the outdoor movies on Saturday nights at a local store ... free, under the stars and a short walk. We received our orders:

"Take a blanket. It gets cold."

"Cold? Mom, I'm boilin'. It was ninety today."

"Listen. It gets cold here when the sun sets."

"A blanket? I'm wearin' my sweatshirt. I'll look stupid with a blanket."

"Have it your way. Mark my words, you'll see."

"Take the Citronella oil," said Aunt Della. "The mosquitoes will eat you alive."

"Citronella? What's that?"

"Rub it all over, even in your hair." I stuffed the bottle into my back pocket.

"And take this flashlight. You'll need it for walking home." She handed me Uncle Carlo's Army flashlight with the light at right angles to the handle. I clipped it to my belt.

Set in a secluded area of the store's grounds, adjacent to an unpaved parking lot, was a white, wooden screen attached to a short post. Above the screen was a cone-shaped speaker. Propped on a table was a two-reel projector. A black wire ran from the projector along the lot to and through a barely open store window.

A murmur welled up. Kids whistled, chanted, "Moo-vie, Moo-vie."

"Ya gotta wait, kids. It's too light out," barked the jumpy projectionist. The sunset.

"Yea! A Bugs Bunny cartoon!" The crowd cheered and then quieted.

The soft light bathing the parking lot and the one streaming from the projector attracted swarms of moths, an army of gnats, and an occasional June bug that droned in like a B-52. A whining buzz tickled my ears ... Zzzzz, zzzzz. I smacked my hand. Splat. Blood! Mosquitoes! Platoons arose from the camouflage of the nearby marsh, attacking like Spitfires, sparing no bare skin.

I whipped the bottle of Citronella from my pocket with the speed of a gunslinger and spread the oil on my face (ugh) neck, hands, and ankles. The smell was nauseating, but not for the mosquitoes. They dove to dine.

A cool breeze from the ocean swept the bugs away for a moment. Beyond the sea, a horn blew rhythmically. The ocean's salty dew landed softly on my face.

My sun-warmed skin was chilled; shivers preceding goosebumps. I rolled down the cuffs of my khakis and snuck my nose further into my Ivory Soap-scented sweatshirt. I wish I had that blanket. I went for a Charleston Chew. The store smelled of popcorn and warmth. At the movie's end, the crowd clapped. Two small floodlights awakened. Car engines rumbled. The foghorn stopped.

What a night! Goosebumps, bites, blood, cold, shivers and all, it was worth every moment. I whipped the flashlight off my belt and flipped it on. "Let's move."

As we ambled back to the cabin, we were accompanied by fireflies under a bright sky with a full moon, brilliant stars, and crashing waves.

A night away from the hot city, at the beach and with a movie. It meant summer.

A Carnival. It Must Be Summer

The Carnival was a happening of the summer season, calling friends, neighbors, and even teachers to gather around the festive sounds and smell that only a carnival can produce. An opening-night parade summoned us to the bright carnival lights and oompah-rhythmic carousel music.

Our carnival was on the grounds of the Saint Vincent de Paul Home overlooking Valley Street and the City of Providence ... a pot just large enough to tuck in the carnival.

Brassy sounds and distant glows painted the horizon, beckoning us as we walked along steamy streets, passing bungalows, three-deckers, and family businesses, one of them Paul's Lemonade Store where, for a nickel, we bought a cup loaded with lemons and iced enough to give us a headache. Glittering lights, music, the merry-go-round, cotton candy, candy apples, booths for games of chance, and raffles welcomed us.

The first rides we saw were the boat swings and a Ferris Wheel. The swings rewarded strength as the boys, fearless, demonstrated how high they could fly, leaning backward, tempting the edges while tugging on knotted ropes. Start low, pull hard, rise on toes, fly high.

When the Ferris Wheel stopped, kids swayed the cars. Workers below cupped their greasy hands and screamed through cigarette-stained teeth, "Hey kids, stop that rockin', or I'll trow yer a** off!"

Around the perimeter were booths for ball tossing (heavy milk bottles, light balls), ring tossing (small rings, large square pegs), games of chance (for losers), spinning wheels (never on my number), and a climbing horse race where the winning prize was a Chinese finger trap. We circled the perimeter, the steady sounds of the carousel's mechanized band playing on autopilot ... oom, pa, pa, oom, pa, pa ... slapping drums, clanging bells, crashing cymbals ... oom, pa, paaa, oom, pa, paaa ...

Surrounding the ticket booth was a stage crowned with lights, and trailers for drinks and food; candied apples, popcorn, whorls of cotton candy, Saugy hot dogs with mustard, pizza, a frozen Charleston Chew, a Creamsicle, Hoodsies (a movie star, inside cover), washed down by an Eclipse drink or a Nehi soda. The mixture of smells was sweet, sour, boiled, doughy, and steamy.

And there were the events. A ten-mile opening night road race attracted the great runners, one of them John Kelly of Boston Marathon fame. "Kelly broke the record tonight, ten miles in 48 minutes," Dad said. Late evening events included wrestling for small people with the great Sonny Boy Cassidy, Irish step dancers, band concerts, accordion ensembles, pie, and watermelon eating contests, boring speakers, apple bobbers, and the final evening's highlight, the car (Chevy) raffle.

We opened and closed the carnival on most nights. There was little match for the anticipation of the first and the sadness of the last. With promises kept and expectations fulfilled, the summer highlight had passed.

I walked home with wonderful memories and ... a Chinese finger trap.

A Summer Love

This week, we watched a movie, *Summer of '42*, that reminded me of a summer love I had so many years ago, No, I did not come of age as did Hermie in the movie. Nonetheless, it rekindled a memory of the summer of '52 when I was thirteen and staying at our rental cottage at the Rhode Island shore.

One evening, as I was playing softball in the small, grassy field in front of our cabin, a girl with blond hair tied in a ponytail ambled along, silhouetted against the sinking sun. I shielded my eyes. She turned, smiled, raised her hand, and scrunched a wave. I looked around. She was waving at me!

I rose to my toes, brushed my sweatshirt, and started a slow walk. I stopped to tighten my belt, then picked up the pace.

She was tall and so pretty. Her eyes were soft and sparkly. Her smile, highlighted by her tan, was wide and bright. I took my hat off and ran my hand over the stubble of my rah-rah. After an inaugural silence, I eked out a "Hi." I was looking for her to run with my opening. She did.

"Hi. I saw you playing." She fiddled with her gimp bracelet. I had a gimp bracelet.

"Oh, yeah, thanks," being among my better responses. I put my right hand in my pocket, the left still in the glove. I looked into her blue eyes.

"What's your name? I'm Ann. I'm staying with a friend. I'll see you tomorrow. Or at the outdoor movies on Saturday. You go to the movies, don't you?"

Meet? The outdoor movies? My favorite. "Yes. I love them." As she turned, her ponytail swung lightly in rhythm with her steps. I ran at top speed back to the game. Uncle Carlo smiled as I sped by.

The next morning, I bounded out of bed, slipped on my bathing suit, skipped breakfast, and hustled to the beach. No Ann. The rest of the week was no different. During the days, I walked the beach, but she was never there. On Saturday evening, I sped to the outdoor movie. Ann was not there either. I never saw her again.

The beach beckoned us by day and captured us by night with its steady cadence of the rising sun, crashing waves, cool breezes, and the moon's reflections. This year, there was more. Something stirred in me for the first time.

At July's end, it was time to return to the city. One evening, I sat on a rock, the infinite rhythm of the ocean ticking like the metronome of music class. It wasn't the melancholy-last-days-of-summer ticking. It was the melancholy ticking off the last days of summer at the beach.

Those days filled me with joy, molding the early days of youth, the memory of a fleeting moment adding even more. From that instant, things started to change.

Those days of long ago happened in a world of crabbing and Noxzema and outdoor movies. Adolescence was somehow more innocent then.

Summer Sunday Morning

I love the summer Sunday mornings when I take my coffee and the New York Times and sit under the umbrella in our rear yard. It's OK that I am frequently interrupted.

Every place I look captures my eyes and my thoughts. Sunrise, framed by a friendly arbor propping up clematis and roses, was peeking over the house in the rear. It is a small carriage house that once was part of our property, sold as three condominiums long before we bought it.

The carriage house has such charm with its angles, cupola, and handsome windows. Steam from my coffee cup made it mystical in the morning light. I wished it were part of our property once again.

For a brief, blunt moment, I picked up my cell phone to retrieve my email, but when I saw the echoes of light on the trees and flowers and heard the songs of the birds, I put it face down on the table. Why spoil these moments?

In the distance, fenced between the arbor and the carriage house, was my garden, bursting with vegetable plants, perennial flowers, and grapes from the arbor. Tucked among them were four fig trees: ready and waiting.

The sounds were all of nature. A nearby hum reminded me of summer days at the shore when I picked up a conch shell and put it to my ear. "Do you hear the ocean, Edward?" I did then, but today's purr was a window air conditioner in the house next door.

A light breeze luffed the umbrella above my head. The nasturtiums reflected yellows and orange; the lavenders loved their pots; the hearty zinnias in delicate pinks, reds, yellows, and greens were finally reaching the sky. The lawn was at ease, topped in two areas by gleaming, silver balls that I kick daily from place to place.

Sunflowers against the house were bending. Daylilies in full bloom meant it was mid-summer. Interspersed were the scattered American flags that Diane had placed.

I was not alone. A hummingbird stopped at the zinnias. The little wren blurted his big sound. Chickadees sang *chickadee-dee-dee.* Here darted a cardinal; there a robin took a bath next to a bird feeder sporting more goldfinch than I had seen in years. In the garden, I spotted the dastardly woodchuck, the one who foraged about my zucchini, winter squash, and pumpkin leaves. He turned confidently, seemed to smile, and sauntered away.

What to do about the woodchuck, now working on my tomatoes? Irish Spring Soap and mothballs stuffed under the shed were no deterrent. Time to call pest control.

Our squirrels are domesticated. They are happy with the birdseed dropping to the ground from the feeders and an occasional buried nut or two. They shop around, gaze at me, and flip their tail to show who the boss is.

From the side of the shed sauntered a confident, calm raccoon.

He darted away when he saw me. I nearly did the same.

Sure, it took all morning to read the *Times*. So what.

Eddie Zack and Campbell's Soup

When I went to the Academy Avenue Elementary School, just a few blocks from our house in Providence, I walked home for lunch. I opened the door to our third-floor tenement on Wealth Avenue and the aroma of the soup, the warmth of our kitchen, and the music greeted me. The soup would be vegetable; the music would be country.

"Edward, would you like some hot Campbell's Vegetable soup with some Tip Top bread and butter?"

"Sure." It was nice that my mother was home at noon. She worked the three-to-eleven shift at The U.S. Rubber Company. At school day's end, my grandmother or aunt, who lived in the tenements below, took over.

The soup was accompanied by music, but not just any music. It was a local group. Mom loved Eddie Zack's Radio Hour ... The Hayloft Jamboree ... broadcast at noon. Yes, we listened to country and western music. Eddie and his robust singing crew ... Cousin Richie, Babs, and Maril, plain resonated country and western.

Eddie did not come from cowboy land. He was homegrown right here in Rhode Island and with an Armenian background to boot. They were the Zackarian family of Providence – Edward (Eddie Zack), his brother Richard (Cousin Richie), and their sisters, Mercedes (Babs) and Marilyn (Maril) – who pioneered the Country & Western music scene in our state and were major players in the introduction of the style into the Northeast. Zack was the founder of the R.I. Country Music Hall of Fame.

The group became a countrywide act, recording for Decca and Columbia, and were the stars of a nationally broadcast NBC radio show originating from WJAR studios in downtown Providence. During the '40s and '50s, they released dozens of successful recordings and were an established major nightclub and concert attraction. The success of The Hayloft Jamboree continued into the 1980s with a string of successful radio and television shows and a series of independent record releases.

We can fast forward to just a couple of summers ago. I saw an ad in the paper for a reunion of the Hayloft Jamboree at the Mishnock Barn in West Greenwich. Well, I could not wait to get there on this warm Sunday afternoon. Diane and I started to swing to the music as soon as we entered. On the stage was Eddie Zack, Jr. rekindling the tunes we heard so many years ago.

The regulars were dressed in wonderful western gear with cowboy boots, tight-fitting jeans, ten-gallon hats, string ties, flowing multicolored dresses, wide belts, and large buckles. Oh my, how they did the Texas two-step so effortlessly. They took no notice of us (me in pale yellow shorts and Nike sneakers) as we danced to "Your Cheatin' Heart" and so many other classic western tunes.

Buttered bread, soup, and western music. What a combo, not only to get back to school in days gone by but also to reawaken those memories on that warm summer day.

The Funnies

I loved the funny papers. Yes, that's what everyone once called the comic strips in the daily newspapers. In the 1920s and through the WWII years, there was a common phrase, "I'll see you in the funny papers," which became a breezy, light-hearted way to say goodbye, see you later; a recognition that lives might be as crazy as the characters in the comics, but at the same time could be funny, ironic, and interesting.

The funnies, daily comic strips with black and white panels of cartoons with compelling captions in balloons, appeared Monday through Saturday on the last page of the evening paper. The Sunday paper had a dedicated section with longer series and with color printing in varied tones.

I'm not sure why, but I read those funnies while kneeling; the paper spread on the linoleum floor in front of the warming Barstow stove, a pale globe above lighting the way, my head resting on my hands cupped under my chin, my fingers straddling my cheeks. The pitter-patter in that busy, doors-always-open, three-story family home may have reached a rumble, but I didn't hear a thing once I became absorbed. My joyful cartoon friends were with me.

The color in the Sunday funnies jumped out even more because they were in their section on the front page of the bulky paper. Those funnies were so good, so appealing, so anticipated. *Tarzan* appeared along with *Terry and the Pirates* and *Buz Sawyer*. Many strips appeared both daily and on Sunday as with *Little Orphan Annie* telling the same story, or *The Phantom,* telling one story in the daily and a different story on Sunday.

As I recall, *Tarzan* and *Buz Sawyer* were on the front page. *Blondie, L'il Abner, Rex Morgan, M.D.,* and *L'il Henry* were all part of the inside establishment. Also, part of the inside crew was the mischievous *Katzenjammer Kids,* two German-American boys with familiar comic-strip iconography such as stars for pain, sawing logs for snoring, speech, and thought balloons. I loved the drawings.

The comic strips also included *Dick Tracy, Little Orphan Annie,* and *Flash Gordon* ... not so humorous, less kid-like, but unfolding an ongoing drama. There were spin-offs of comic books like *Superman, Batman,* and *The Amazing Spider-Man*. Prophetically, in later years, I grew to love one such comic and funny, *Rex Morgan, M.D.*

Imprinted in memory, the comic books and the funnies became an encompassing part of my life. I had a Superman shirt and a Dick Tracy watch with Tracy's rocking gun the second hand. I even clipped some comics and hung, rather taped, them on my bedroom wallpaper.

Mom wasn't happy. Later, I saw Broadway shows like *Annie* and *L'il Abner* which were based on their comics.

We are all linked to a time, a place, a memory. In this case, it was the funnies on the floor, in front of the stove, that afforded such a sweet road of childhood.

"I'll see you in the funny papers."

My First Job: Paperboy

Dad peered over his paper one day and said, "President Truman was a paperboy." I got the message. No, not to be a President, but rather to "Start saving for college," recollecting that he never had the chance for high school education. So, I became a paperboy.

Every afternoon, I went to the depot and, at tables abuzz with eager newspaper carriers, stacked the papers in my *Journal-Bulletin* bag, and draped it along my right side to just above the knee. I delivered *The Providence Journal's Evening Bulletin* to sixty-five families.

Collecting money was challenging and fun, especially at Christmas when I made fifty dollars in tips. The cost of the daily and Sunday papers was forty-five cents. Customers flipped me a fifty-cent piece and said, "Keep the change, kid." With my pay of one penny per paper per day, five cents for Sundays, I averaged ten dollars a week and, at school, I added the money to my Old Stone Bank account.

Collection day was Saturday. I had a coin dispenser like the trolley conductor's, with slots for quarters, dimes, nickels, and pennies. Fast enough, I flicked my thumb and the change dropped into the fingers of the same hand. I made change for a dollar with a flick, flick, slide, and flick, and there it was fifty-five cents. "Gimme fifty." I slipped the nickel into my right pocket. Tips did not belong in any slot.

Most of the customers were genuinely nice. I remember one stop when, after knocking, I heard the slapping of cards, the clinking of ice in glasses, the scrape of a moving chair, and then, silence. I paused as I heard gorilla feet thump across the kitchen in two steps. A giant in slippers opened the door. With a comforting smile and his hand on my shoulder, he said, "Hi, kid. Come in. C'mon. Come in." I had never seen him in the neighborhood.

I hesitated, stepped gently over the threshold, and entered a dark kitchen where I spotted card players who suffered my intrusion, having laid down their cards. The brightest thing in the room was the stark white icebox in a corner; a puddle beneath it. A dog growled from behind a closed door.

I flashed a sidelong glance at the slightly ajar doorway, slouched, and put a foot in the entry. "Wait, wait, son. Wanna Coke?"

"No, thanks."

He handed me fifty cents. "Keep the change. See ya next week."

"Thank you." Whistling, I hustled down the stairs two at a time.

There were good tippers and poor tippers. Some called me a cute kid and those who never spoke.

There were houses with dirty stairs and houses with clean stairs. There were smells of cabbage, cigarettes, cigars, meatballs, old wood, Lysol, sweat, dust, mold, wine, damp cellars, and onions frying.

There were sounds of kids crying, people arguing, tenors practicing, dishes rattling, and radios blaring a Red Sox game.

I smelled of newspaper ink and loved it.

My Paper Route on Health Avenue

Among the many things that made my paper route so much fun was the street where I delivered the papers. Health Avenue in Providence, Rhode Island, was part of a trilogy with Wealth (my street) and Wisdom Avenues and harbored a cultural treasure of community. As the paperboy, I was part of it.

It was a conventional city street flanked by comfortably spaced bungalows and two- or three-family homes whose doorways opened directly onto the sidewalks. There was a rare lawn and a few garages. On its only vacant lot, we could take on a role as a football or baseball player, or an Army commando.

Sturdy curbstones supported cement sidewalks, embedded at regular intervals with commemorative plates acknowledging the WPA workers who built them. My grandfather was one, and I still feel a sense of pride whenever I unexpectedly come across one of these plaques.

The sidewalks were dotted with rows of tall telephone poles shaped in the letter "T" and linked by sloping lines. Streetlights were suspended from the middle of the poles and were covered with round scalloped, swaying metal hats. They emitted a yellow haze which created dancing shadows on the street. Those lights became our summer evening clocks. A netless basketball rim was nailed onto a pole, one which also might be used as a goal in hide and seek.

Health Avenue was perpendicular to the main thoroughfare, Academy Avenue. Its beginning was bracketed by two imposing three-family houses and its end was marked by two more that looked over and down the street. Cars and houses were never locked. There were no broken windows. Nothing dreadful ever happened, but something was always happening.

On snow days, the residents shoveled, making piles of snow that were an open invitation for climbing, tunneling, and walking atop their length. Narrow paths were cleared just enough to negotiate.

Everyone received the newspaper. There seemed no other choice, not that they would make one. I hustled through the route quickly for two reasons. I wanted to please my customers with prompt delivery. And I wanted to spend more of my after-school time playing with friends.

I delivered the evening edition of *The Providence Journal-Bulletin* every day after school, and in the morning on Saturday and Sunday. I believe it was necessary, certainly for me, for a neighborhood kid to deliver the paper. It might be a solitary activity, but in going from house to house, I got to know so much about my customers. I ran up the stairs with piston-rod legs, tossed a folded paper, and even more quickly scooted back down. But when I entered the homes on collection days, I was involved.

I shared their common, everyday lives. I learned their idiosyncrasies – don't throw the paper, place it gently on the front step, hit the door so I know it's here, come in and put it on the table. Theirs were part of my identity.

Next week, you will learn more about those customers.

The Folks On My Paper Route

Even though my customers were my neighbors, I learned so much more with the route. Sure, I met them in church, at the movies, in the stores, and on the streets, but now, I saw them in their homes. Italians, Irish, Poles, Scots, and English; a potpourri of neighborhood professors who educated me.

There was the man with big jowls and smooth, yellow skin that looked like tile. I thought he had a 'gland' problem. There was a man who was wheelchair-bound. I opened his door every day to place his paper on the table next to him. He was alone. His wife was working. He liked to talk. I liked to run, but I didn't.

There were four schoolteachers; one I had in the third grade. There was a regal priest. There was the man who hid behind his house when I walked by. There was a future mayor and a future governor. There were two tenors; one who sang in the local church, the other who sang in Madison Square Garden.

There was a college hockey player and an all-state track star. There was a Holy Cross All-American football player, now a school principal.

There was Phil who everyone called Jimmy Hagan because he liked golf, even though the golfer was Walter Hagan. There was a noble man who wore a smoking jacket and cradled a Bocchino (holder) for his cigarette.

There were my friends' parents. There were girlfriends. There was our iceman who knew of Nap Lajoie, the Hall-of-Famer from Woonsocket. There was an Air Force pilot. There was a firefighter. There was a nurse.

There was a tall man in a short bathrobe. There was a short man in shorts. There was a man with a twitch.

There was a cat woman with a nasal twang. There was a nasal woman with a cat twang. There were dog lovers and dog haters. There were mean dogs and nice dogs.

There was the Scot who was a soccer star. There was the family that owned a restaurant. There was a market and a liquor store.

I loved my route, though Sundays were a challenge. The paper was much larger because of a magazine insert and the extra ads. My Radio Flyer red wagon was near toppling when I loaded it at the paper store. I was alone because Louie, my helper, was an altar boy. Mom – Peter, go help him. Dad – He'll be fine.

One early Sunday morning, delivering alone with no one in sight, I thought I heard a baby crying. While looking for the sound and the help of an adult, I ended up behind a garage, where I scared a crying cat.

Some of my customers became my patients years later. How challenging it was to change roles, me now their advisor. But caring for them was so much easier because they were so familiar.

The paper route enriched my link to our neighborhood and its people. What a great education.

CHAPTER II

NEIGHBORHOOD

A Snow Man and a Snow Fort

The first snowfall of the year reminds me of my boyhood days of snowball fights, sledding, snowmen, and a snow fort. Now, except for an occasional snowman, I do none of it. I don't want to fight, sledding is too dangerous, the cold is too penetrating, and I'd prefer to leave snow fort construction to our children for our grandchildren. I'll watch *Frosty the Snow Man*.

Snow was so much more fun when we were kids, especially when school was canceled. I started the day by dressing in dungarees (finally shedding the snowsuit), a wool shirt, a sweatshirt, a heavy coat, two pairs of heavy socks covered by black boots with four almost impossible-to-buckle clasps (I tucked my pants), a toque, and gloves. Now, I was ready for the snowman and the snow fort. Just out the door, I made a snow angel by lying down in the fresh powder, extending my arms and legs as far as I could and then moving them up and down, side to side.

Hoping for slightly moist snow so that I could roll it like a stone, I started the snowman by packing a snowball and pushing it about the yard as the heavy snow stuck. The big ball would stand where I could push no further. Back I went for the torso, starting a little closer so the next roll would be smaller and liftable. Back for the head, ending with something easier to lift. I packed snow into the gaps to round the sides. It may have been a bit lopsided, but it was done! Now, I understand there are battery-powered perfect snow spheres that attract snow by an electrical charge forming the body of a snowman. No way! A real snowman must be rolled, packed, and sealed with love.

To the cellar for coal to make the eyes, mouth, and buttons, to the kitchen for a carrot nose, to my bedroom for an old hat and a scarf. Some sticks from the yard for skinny arms.

And now for the snow fort. We needed protection from enemy snowballs flying across the street. We made the fort by packing mounds of snow in a circle and then trying to make a roof, to no avail. Nevertheless, it afforded enough protection for the fight. We had stacked a bunch of perfect snowballs behind the fort, but as the fight got going, we ran out and simply smashed snow in our hands to throw in rapid-fire, like a Gatling gun. Fight over. Everybody won.

Wet frozen toes and fingers, windburned cheeks, and chapped lips forced us to the warmth of home. Now exhausted, cold, and hungry we awaited Mom's hot cocoa and something more that I loved … Campbell's Vegetable Soup and Tip Top Bread with hunks of butter, easily dunkable.

What is great about snow? Why, everything.

Time to make a snowman and a snow fort. Time for cocoa and soup.

Bullied, I Guess

I never thought of it as bullying. I just thought that older and bigger meant stronger, tougher, and thus meaner.

Two thugs came to the Academy Avenue Elementary School yard at recess and demanded "protection money." They looked like the kids in the Bowery Boys movies, but without the slapstick.

"You. C'mere. If ya want pratekshun, ya gotta give us a nickel or we'll kill ya."

"The nickel is for my snack at the Variety Store."

"A nickel or we'll kill ya. And dunt tell yer fatha." I learned years later that their dark sides continued; one had his fingers blown off by a cherry bomb. The other was serving time for murder. Good thing I yielded the nickel.

There was a second episode, different. It was a beautiful late fall day with a few hours of daylight remaining. As I left the school, I walked along Academy Avenue when she bounded out of the hedges, yanked my Navy toque, a regular target for a steal and throw, and threw it in the tree. I was also wearing my dark blue Pea jacket, one worn by sailors when the fog was as thick as pea soup. It had broad lapels and a collar that, when pushed up, covered my face up to the toque. I loved the way it protected me from the wind and cold.

I knew of her. I wanted to be her friend. Fright will make you try the best friend route. We were wearing the same pea jacket. She rolled her fist into a ball. "What are you doing here?"

"Here?"

"Yah. You heard me."

"Walking. Home. I live, uhhh, there." I made a blunt point with my free elbow.

"By my street?"

Why me? I followed all the rules that should keep me out of a fight ... diminutive, quiet, innocent, and non-combative. To top it off, I was wearing the jacket that I thought made me invincible.

This time I wanted it to make me invisible. The following words came to mind: pummel, punch, pound, maul, kick, and blood.

Even the greatest in my neighborhood unraveled to silence when they were scared. I was now in the silent world of someone who was about to be pounded. She tightened her fist around the collar, pulled me closer, looked me in the face, dry nose to wet nose, and, spewing a bit of spittle, told me to "Screw."

No problem. 'Screw.' Such a beautiful word. I was off like a scared rabbit, feet pounding, sucking air, and pumping arms. I made the corner, turned up my street, and was home in seconds, puffing out steam.

Mom. "Where's your hat?"

"I left it in school?"

"Be sure to get it tomorrow. Why are you puffing?" The toque was something to worry about later. I was happy to be alive. I ignored the puffing question.

I saw her over the years, being sure to avoid her though she was now smaller and seemed kinder.

I wonder what happened to that toque.

Wireless in Rhode Island

Diane and I heard that there was a monument dedicated to the inventor of the wireless telegraph, Guglielmo Marconi, in Roger Williams Park, so off we went to find it. I was especially interested since we had visited the Marconi Museum in Chatham, Massachusetts; a fascinating place to learn about the beginning of wireless and the use of Morse code.

The Rhode Island monument to Marconi is an eighteen-foot shaft of granite nestled in a copse of trees on a knoll off Frederick Greene Boulevard, about one hundred yards south of Providence's Carr Street.

A handsome and fitting testimonial to the Nobel Prize winner, it sat overlooking a tranquil pond. Its beauty and power were striking.

At the Providence Public Library, I found stories of its inception in a 1953 *Providence Journal*.

Work for the monument started before WWII in 1937. It was halted when the United States broke off diplomatic relations with Italy at the start of the war. Completed granite pieces were stored in Westerly and Providence.

A committee of undeterred citizens ... Walter F. Fitzpatrick, Oresto DiSaia, Frank Rao, and Ms. Alice Thompson, with advice from Luigi Scala and broadcaster Antonio Pace, moved forward after the war to get the Roger Williams site approved.

The monument was dedicated on October 26, 1953, with Marconi's proud daughter, Degna Paresce, the guest of honor. "I am honored and pleased," she said while standing at the foot of the monument. A host of other state and religious dignitaries were present, one of whom, Bishop McVinney, expressed the hope that Marconi's invention would be used for the good of mankind. Senators Pastore and Greene said it was fitting for the monument to be in Roger Williams Park as both men – Guglielmo Marconi and Roger Williams – were described as pioneers. Marvelous.

Guess what! There is another Marconi monument in Cranston, R.I. Diane and I found it at the corner of Atwood and Plainfield Streets in the Knightsville section, close to St. Rocco's Church. It stands unrecognized and lonely under nearby traffic lights at a busy intersection. Only a few seemed interested when Diane was taking pictures. This monument was dedicated in 2001 and Marconi's youngest daughter, Elettra, was in attendance.

I wonder what Marconi would think today if he saw where the wireless world has come. I thought about the Bishop's comment ... used for the good of mankind. May we continue to hope?

As you all know and have heard me say at my presentations, "I believe it is good to remember and record the past. It is good to recognize those who have contributed. It is good to acknowledge genius. It is good to erect lasting monuments."

Guglielmo Marconi, a humble and kind man, typified the "spirit of the good heart and genius for work." If you are in Roger Williams Park or nearby Cranston, find the Marconi monuments. Pause for a moment to appreciate his genius. Applaud those who acknowledged his accomplishments in perpetuity.

Life Lessons from a Pinball Machine

On occasion, during a lazy afternoon while on summer vacation, I played the pinball machine at Abe's Variety Store across the street from my old elementary school. Abe went home for lunch and reopened at one. Head down, melancholy, he murmured something, unlocked the door, groaned it open, and did not look up until he gave me my Chunky and my change.

Abe was a small, pale, balding man with a stubble of a beard. He wore frameless glasses like Melville's *Bartleby, the Scrivener*. Though slight and thin, he wore suspenders.

I loved the Chunky; a dense pyramid square, a rhomboid (now in junior high, I had taken geometry) of chocolate loaded with nuts, cashews, and raisins. Abe stored his candy behind a smoky, glass counter next to the gumball machine. On this quiet summer day, I gave him my quarter, he returned four nickels and the Chunky. I strolled across the oily, buckled floor to a machine tucked in the corner against the window, stood behind the controls ... flippers, plunger, and spring, and for a moment I draped my hands over the sides, slid them up and down along the smooth, worn wood, caressed the flippers' buttons and paused.

I reached into my pocket and pulled a nickel. Near the plunger was a little door with a lock where the nickels dropped. I stared at the glass ahead; the command center that displayed points flashed lights and made noises ... knuk, knuk, knuk ... for bonus games.

Nickel in ... blurt, bang, ring-a-ding, ding, bop, blurp, a sound deep within of silver balls dropping ... one, two, three, four, five. I pushed the plunger and into the slot arose the first smooth, shiny beauty.

I pulled the springer back, held it there a moment, and finally let go, shooting the ball, cannon-like up the right side to the uppermost curve where in slow motion it straddled the bend along the top, stopped, and made its descent. The silver beauty zigged, zagged, and picked up speed as it moved down the slant of the table. It fell into holes ... bing, bing ... and popped out ... ka-ching ... as if shot from a cannon, ricocheted through a thicket of wickets, bumpers, and poles that lit up when hit, racking up points along its way while heading toward my flippers.

Flashes of electrical energy, lights, chimes, bells, and buzzers meant more points and more points meant free games! At the bottom, dead in the middle, was the cavernous, dreaded drain, the sinkhole into oblivion where eventually all balls disappeared, the widespread flippers no longer able to protect. I rocked the machine when Abe was not watching, but the predictable tilt foiled me.

Abe's was a training ground where I learned that pinball was a little like life ... wins and losses, chances to win again, replays, tilts that should be avoided, manageable disappointment.

Was the trip to Abe's and the challenge worth it? You bet. There was always the Chunky.

Trolleys on the Avenue

I was asked recently if I remembered trolleys from my youth. Some years ago, I wrote an article thereof, so I am taking the opportunity to revisit it.

The electric trolleys were masses of powerful metal tethered with poles to wires above that supplied the energy needed for gliding, rumbling, and wobbling along their tracks while passing rows of merchants: the tailor, shoemaker, barber, grocer, the undertaker, baker, saloon keeper, liquor store owner, and fish-man.

Academy Avenue was a busy neighborhood street where people bustled along sidewalks and streetcars hummed along the street. Trolley tracks and overhead wires connected one end to the other; the trolley's poles swaying underwires that looked like giant spider webs.

The trolley was more than a ride. It was an adventure. Sometimes I saw a dead mouse crushed in the tracks and wondered what a cat would look like … or a dog. Or half my foot. I purposely caught my shoe in the track.

Dad, in a rare moment of defiance and bravery when no trolley or autos were in sight, smirked, "Watch me drive the Chevy on the tracks. Do you feel us gliding, Edward? How she slides so smoothly?" He was excited, but just as quickly as he got on the tracks, he got off but loved his moment of mischief. On a face that would have tightened in disapproval if he knew what we did with the trolleys, he now had a wispy smile of triumph. I tried it with my bike, but the wheels got stuck in the track.

It was the older kids who pulled the big adventures. I might put caps in the tracks to hear the rat-a-tat-tat. That was it. But those guys tried the formidable cherry bomb which might, we thought, jolt the car near off the track. In my trusty Keds, I buzzed by the bakery and hid behind the building to hide. This wasn't blind man's bluff or Red Rover. This was the real thing. But the cherry bomb fizzled.

The real thrill was when they ran after the car, jumped, and pulled the boom off the wire. Screech…the sound of the untethered trolley coming to an abrupt powerless halt. Down the steps and around to the rear came the mumbling conductor to reattach the boom. "Damn kids!"

They dug up the tracks one day and replaced them with a smooth, black street. Gone were the rumbles, clickety clacks, and screeches. Gone was another neighborhood institution. I didn't need much more to bond me to the neighborhood because I lived, learned, and played there, but the trolley was among the favorites.

I drove to Atwells and Academy avenues recently. I visualized the trolley following the streets of my youth where we found fun, friendship, and familiarity.

Now, so many years later, I think about those distant scenes. As time passes, I grow more nostalgic for the memories of youth. Though the trolley and the tracks are long gone, their image remains.

Wait ... was that a screech I heard?

Do You Come to Providence?

I went to my barber last week, following which I took my usual stroll through Wayland Square in Providence. I have been going there for years; when I lived nearby and now when I come into Providence from our home in Bristol. I like Wayland Square ... neat shops, the bookstore, the coffee shop, a nice sandwich shop, people and students milling and talking around.

I strolled from the dangerous attraction of Books on the Square and was heading to a coffee shop when I turned the corner and bumped into Bernie, a longtime friend (I have no old friends). I had not seen him in a while. He was as refined, dignified, and engaging as always. It was so nice to see him. When you see a friend you have not seen in some time, there is a gap easily bridged. We caught up quickly.

We chatted, making eye contact, pleased that here we were in our eighth decade and still busy, active – he especially so, chairing an important board. We had rarely crossed paths in our professional careers, but we shared a bond of having our forefathers come from the same town in Italy in the late 19th and early 20th centuries. What remarkable opportunities they afforded us.

Appreciating that history, Bernie said, "We need to catch up, have lunch one day. Where are you living?"

"Sure. I would love to. Bristol. I've been in Bristol for twenty-five years."

"Oh yeah, right." And then he asked a question that reflected our prevailing provincialism. "Do you get to Providence often?"

Chuckling, I replied, "Well, sure, of course, I do, Bernie. Here I am," I paused, realizing that yes, I come to Providence, but not as regularly as I once did. When I do, I combine bunches of things. Today, it was the barber, the bookstore, and a weekly lunch with friends for a conversation with an Italian professor. How funny. Only a few miles away, and I come only of necessity. These days, I like to stay in the East Bay.

"We should have lunch or at least a coffee." He uttered those magic words ... lunch, coffee. It was good because I like to meet with friends, especially those I have not seen in a while, to catch up and explore new ideas. It wasn't about eating or drinking. It was about talking, sharing, commiserating, and looking to the future. Yes, we were busy senior citizens with more to do, much to accomplish. In no way did we, or could we, dwell on being seniors. But ...

"Bernie, it's hard to believe we've gotten to this age. When my father was fifty, I thought he was old. And, you know what, he was."

'Yes, yes, I agree," Bernie replied. "We'll have much to share. I'll be in touch."

How nice. I am looking forward to our meeting and spending some time with this gentleman friend.

Lucky for me that I turned the corner.

Bring Back the Peddler

With a quarantine upon us, I wonder what it would be like to have our neighborhood peddlers back. Trusted men who added life to our streets, they rumbled down Wealth Avenue in waves.

Joe the ragman was a musty unshaven, gnome-like character who wore a long gray, tattered coat buttoned to the top, and a small, visored matching hat. His squeaky, horse-drawn cart was laden with stacks of rags that smelled of the dampness of a cellar. He gurgled "Rraggs," with a nasal twang. When summoned, up the stairs he plodded on dilapidated dirty boots, satchel over his shoulder.

The fisherman's dark-green, open, panel truck transported firm, fresh fish arranged in wooden sections fitted to the bed of the truck. A rattling scale on a chain hung from a hook. Melting ice dripped from the tailgate. Unshaven and wearing a discolored old Yankee cap tipped to the side, he bore the vaporous look of exhaustion. His canvas coat was stained with dried blood. His high rubber boots flopped against his knees. He grabbed the fillet, flipped it onto the scale, wrapped it in newspaper, and off he went, the engine rumbling.

The waffle man (yep, we did) wore a white apron and a tall white hat. He drove a red truck with smooth round fenders and small wheels. After parking, he arose from his low seat and stepped to the raised rear platform, taking his place behind his waffle grilles. As he slid open the window, the aroma of oil and frying dough drifted out. "Yes?" "Two waffles with extra powdered sugar, please," we chirped.

The iceman stepped from the running board, shuffled to the rear, threw a leather protector onto his back and, lifting tongs from a hook, grabbed a thick block of ice, slung it onto his shoulder and, body rounded by its weight, carried it up the stairs. With drops of water splashing off the heels of his wrinkled, waterlogged boots that squeaked as if he were walking in the snow, he thumped up the stairs.

The ice cream man was a fragile, wiry, frenetic guy who drove a Humpty Dumpty truck that looked like an armored car. Drumsticks, Popsicles, and Creamsicles appeared from a freezer tucked into the rear.

The laundryman picked up the dirty clothes in a sack, loaded them into his large brown truck, and a week later returned with a neat package wrapped in brown paper.

The Cushman Bakery man, smartly dressed in a tan-striped shirt and brown pants, sold the best chocolate layer cake.

The milkman gave us chunks of ice to suck on hot days. He sprinted from the passenger side door with his basket of milk and eggs, returning with empties on the way out.

The clothing man drove an old Buick with a trunk packed with suits, shirts, ties, and coats. Hair pomaded, dressed in a three-piece suit, he looked around, moved quickly, and never spoke.

There was an umbrella man, a knife sharpener, and a vegetable seller; wandering merchants who played in the orchestra of my neighborhood.

Would that they were here today.

I Was Always a Hobo

Our quiet, level Bristol street is a welcoming one for trick or treaters. Diane and I love to see the eager, costumed little kids prance to the door and stand fast to the cries of nearby parents, "Go ahead and ring it. Go ahead."

They ring the bell, and we swing the door open to the squeaks of "Trick-or-Treat."

Because we live near Roger Williams College, we get several undergraduates stepping up to fill their coffers, some costumed, most not. One late evening, as we dimmed the lights thinking the kids were long gone, there came a knock. Standing there were four large young men 'adorned' with cooks' uniforms. "What are you guys supposed to be?"

"Cooks."

"You are cooks! Don't you work in that restaurant right down the street?"

"Well ... uh, yeah ... but."

"OK, here you go."

In my early years, when fall and the cool, dark nights descended on our Mt. Pleasant neighborhood, we thought of Halloween.

We were excited to get out of school and get costumed up, roaming about with friends, candy spinning in our heads. Halloween was an evening of enthusiasm, excitement, and expectation. In the days, weeks, before, the questions were "What are you going to be for Halloween?" or "What will the trick be if we don't get a treat?"

Our costumes were homemade; a ghost with a sheet over the head and eyelets, a scarecrow with straw tucked in the sleeves of an old shirt, an old lady with a housedress, a hobo (my choice), fashioned with a tattered, oversized coat and a fire-charred cork smeared on my face.

Wandering along with pillowcases ready, off we went with a group of friends that gathered under the streetlight. The wintry night air was vibrant with kids. Gibbering chatter filled the streets. We hoofed from door to door through the shadows with street and porch lights guiding our way.

Three-decker houses made it easier. Up the rear stairs we lumbered, our loads weightier at each landing. People welcomed us with a smile, a pleasant greeting, and a handful of candy … Reece's Peanut Butter Cups, M&M's, Mr. Goodbar, Hershey Chocolates, Charleston Chew, and Butterfingers. The neighborhood was thrumming with the sights and sounds of kids and the aromas of candy.

We never came up empty, so there was never a trick to deploy but for wax. Except for the slingshot or a bean blower, candlewax was the most dangerous weapon we ever carried, not to light the way, but to wax car and storefront windows. And wax we did, so much on the store windows that you could not see in, or out.

At the end of the evening, I shuffled the three flights of stairs to our tenement lugging a full pillowcase by my grandmother's second floor where she was standing and quipped, "Edward, you must-a be tired inna the legs."

The muscles of my tormented face were frozen by the charcoal, but I was able to smile.

What a night!

The Bell of the Ice Cream Truck

It was a sound clear enough to hear miles away; the tingling bell of the ice cream truck that ambled along, street to street, stop and go, laden with its rich treats. It arrived after supper. "Finish your meal or I won't give you the nickel, Edward."

Herbie, the Humpty Dumpty man, was a short-statured, serious frenetic guy like Alice's Mad Hatter. He had a hook-shaped nose and owl eyes set back in his small face. He sold the ice cream from an armored freezer that was sitting on the rear deck of his panel truck, adroitly pulling the order without looking.

When he arrived, we were standing by the curb with money in hand, thinking of the myriad of delicious treats inside and ever puzzled about which to get.

Across the front of the truck, from the top of the windshield to the freezer, was a buttoned-down, soft canvas cover. There were no doors. As he squeaked to a stop, I thought of Drumsticks, Popsicles, and ice cream sandwiches, but this night I could taste the smooth Creamsicle, an orange Popsicle covering a vanilla ice cream center.

Dan came out of his house eating an apple. When he saw Herbie's truck, he tossed the half-eaten apple high, such that it landed on the canvas cover.

I strolled to the truck planning to punch the canvas to launch the apple into the air. My timing was perfect. As I approached the passenger side and launched the punch, Herbie had turned in his seat and, hunched over, exited that same side. I hit something soft. I backed away to look for the flying apple, but it was nowhere in sight. Rather, I saw Herbie with his hand over his eye. I realized then what had happened. I had punched him! "He's coming after me."

He paused, stunned, surprised, and motionless.

"What the heck did you do that for?"

"What?"

"Punch me!"

"I didn't punch you!" I turned to an audience of friends squirming, bent, smuggling a laugh. "I was trying to punch the apple on the canvas. I didn't know you would come out at the same time on the same side. I'm sorry."

"Aw, baloney!"

By now, my friends were rolling with laughter. "No more ice cream, ever, for me," I thought. I would be lucky to live, never mind eat. With his hand over his eye, Herbie walked to the rear of the truck, opened the freezer door, and took out a Creamsicle which replaced his hand. He glared at me with the other eye.

"What the hell do you want?"

"Uh, uh, uh ... a Creamsicle? ... puh ... please."

"Sure, what else! Sonofabitch. Man, this hurts."

He took my nickel and zoomed away; one bell rung, the other fading.

Herbie returned the following evening. I hid behind a maple tree, peeking and bobbing like a pigeon. He exited the driver's side. His eye was black. I shuffled to the truck. He glared. "What?"

"Uh, I'll have a Drumstick."

CHAPTER III

PARENTS

What Do You Keep of Your Parents' Belongings?

Diane and I are in the not-so-easy process of downsizing. While we are not yet ready to move from our comfortable home in Bristol, we can see the day is nearing. As we begin the process of taking a good look at all we have, I am reminded of the days after my parents were gone.

There were many wistful and sad moments as my brother and I and our families sorted through our parents' belongings. Trying to hold on to bygone days made everything more difficult as we were immersed in memories and emotion. We found things that once, barely registering, were now treasures.

It was hard to let go of even the merest, an ashtray from their New York honeymoon, Dad's billfold, a set of keys, an old watch, vases, and wall hangings from forever ago and a drawer full of Mom's scarves. Each book, each article of clothing, furniture, everything, represented a memory.

We had to make quick decisions because it felt as if we were doing something terrible. It took courage. It became easier as we sat at the table where we had so many Sunday dinners and joked about Mom's ravioli and chicken croquettes.

We sorted through pictures going back to when they were young, before they were married … before we were a family. Dad, dressed as if he were in a Gatsby movie, Mom, a flapper. There was no way to tell they were working people and not Hollywood stars.

We weren't decluttering. We were remembering. We wanted everyone to remember, so we asked relatives to come by to see what clothes of our mother's they might want. We made it a social experience. The huge pile that we left on the table disappeared in an afternoon. Female family and friends were comforted with Mom's clothes, some never worn, tags still hanging. The younger men in the family loved Pop's age-old tools. It gave us all a chance to laugh, sometimes to cry, with delight.

So, what's the use of keeping things just to have them? Well, there is a reason. Because we are responsible for keeping memories alive. What did we keep? Well, some of the classic furniture, some insignificant things, like diaries as reminders of our grandparents' immigration, their early days in America and, of course, the pictures.

Diane and I thought of our 'stuff.' What would our children keep? Would they care about the letters I saved from friends, teachers, mentors, organizations? What about my neckties? Diane's cookbooks? Her china and pottery ware are treasures. Most of what we own has a practical use: chairs, tables, tools, pots, and pans … things that provide a lifetime of comfort harboring memories of family, challenging work, play, and hobbies. Our children don't want that stuff. They have theirs.

We're sifting through a boatload of things, trying to figure out how to dispense of what we can part with now.

We walk by our family's timeworn furniture, sometimes sliding a finger along the edge. We look at the old pictures. They provide an indefinable comfort.

I wonder what our children will keep.

What's Your Favorite Number?

I was at the gas station recently and noted the number plate on the car in front of me, 429. Aha, three digits! That had to be a legacy number, surely with a story behind it, as only a Rhode Islander would understand. 429 has an important back story for me. A casual bettor, Dad often said, "My number came out today. 429. That's the time you were born, Ed, 4:29 AM, and I have hit it at least six times over the years."

I remember many a late summer evening when Dad took me to downtown Providence to "Go get *The Record.*" *The Record* was a Boston newspaper that was delivered to Rhode Island late in the evening. We drove to the corner of Washington and Aborn Streets in downtown Providence where there was a White Tower Diner and a fellow standing in front selling the paper. Dad gave me the money (I'm guessing a nickel), and I handed it to the gentleman who efficiently snap-folded the paper and gave it to me with a "Thanks, kid." Every older friend of my Dad's called me "kid," as did this paper man.

Dad scooted, distancing the car behind to pull over as soon as he could, opened the paper to the rear section, and looked for "the number." "What's the number, Dad?"

"It has to do with the horse races, the first three horses' positions in the last column …" and then he lost me. Most of the time, he said "Dammit." I knew that meant he lost. I was never with him on the rare occasion when he won.

Dad's other favored number, now mine, was four. One year, Diane and I went to the Kentucky Derby; a marvelous experience and spectacle humming with excitement. "Put twenty on the four-horse," Dad said as his eyes widened, recalling the days of *'The Record.'*

I had played the number four horse in a previous race. Knowing nothing about racing, I figured I had as good a chance as any of the other one hundred thousand people there. I won three hundred dollars!

Well, after a long day of many races and lots of waiting, the Derby was off. Dad's horse struggled. When I returned home, Dad, who watched the race on TV, said, "I saw my four-horse get nuzzled, jammed, into the starting gate with a big push by the handlers, but I never saw him again. What the heck happened?"

The horses had started together, but it didn't take long for a separation. The other horses seemed not to like the four-horse, so they somehow found a way to keep him boxed in. That's where he finished. Dead last.

"Dad, he started last and stayed that way all the way around. The other horses almost lapped him."

"The bum," Dad's common refrain when he was unhappy with the performance of an athlete. "No wonder they had to push him in."

Dad Handles the Asbestos

Some years ago, we lived in a large, old house on the East Side of Providence. As is wont to happen in old houses, things broke and this late winter, it was our boiler. It cracked and sprung a leak.

Because we lived in a large home, we needed a boiler large enough to heat it, and this baby was huge. The plumber estimated that it would cost quite a bit to replace it. "I just can't carry it out in one piece from this cave of a cellar. I must disassemble it and reassemble the new one. It will take a while to get the parts. I can pour some oatmeal in the burner to get you through the rest of the winter."

"Oatmeal? Are you crazy? I'll wait." When I heard the final price, I nearly cracked like a boiler.

"Oh, and by the way, one other thing." Uh, oh, here comes more.

"Ya got asbestos lining this place and it needs to be removed. I can't do it. Ya need an expert asbestos removal company. And that's gonna cost ya."

Oh dear. I called the asbestos removal company who estimated the cost at two thousand dollars. "Are you kidding?" I blurted. "The room is only ten by ten by ten."

"Yeah, I know, but we have to put on these special white suits to remove it and then we gotta dispose of it the right way. And that ain't cheap." Stunned, I had little choice.

To be sure the boiler price estimate was correct, I called my father and asked him to bring his eighty-year-old retired plumber friend to check on the price. "Oh, and one other thing, Dad. We can't do anything until I get the asbestos out, and that will cost."

"OK, Ed. I'll come by with Sal." Why was every plumber I knew named Sal? In fact, many Sal's prevailed in my life, Sal the barber, Sal the cleaner, Sal the cook, now Sal the plumber.

I went home that evening, checked the cellar area only to find that the asbestos was gone. The walls were bare. The space was ready for a new boiler. What!? I called my father. "Dad, did you come by today with Sal?"

"Yes. He thought that the price for the boiler was pretty good, and you should go ahead."

"Thanks. But, but, where's the asbestos?"

"The asbestos? Aw, we just ripped it all out. Those guys are nuts charging all that money just because they put on those silly suits."

"That's illegal. Are you guys nuts?"

"Forget it, Ed. We're old. We're not gonna get that cancer."

"I understand that Dad. But what did you do with the asbestos? It has to be disposed of correctly and safely."

"They're nuts (a common refrain of Dad's when he disagreed with something) with that too. We just rolled it up and Sal took care of it when he got home."

My goodness.

Mom and Dad Loved Coffee

I read a splendid review article *Coffee, Caffeine, and Health* by Drs. van Dam, Hu, and Willett in the July 23rd issue of *The New England Journal of Medicine*. It immediately recalled my mother, who drank so much coffee every day that she was called Coffee Benny. I asked my Dad, who was not far behind in consumption, "Why Coffee Benny?" He mentioned something about a local business of the same name. Of that, I cannot be sure. Of the rivers of coffee, I am sure.

For my parents, coffee was about three things: the coffee pot, the thermos and something social. Their coffee pot was a wobbly metal percolator perched on the stove in perpetuity. "Watch the coffee, Peter. Be sure it does not boil over." And so often it did. They ran to the first hiss, often to no avail. A mess of grinds and water doused the gas flame and hopes for a perfect brew. They somehow made the remains drinkable.

They carried sizeable thermos bottles in their lunches. The caffeine kept Dad going as he was up daily at 4:30 AM. For Mom, it contributed to her already hyperactive behavior. She worked in Providence. She started for work running for the bus in the early morning. On her lunch hour, with coffee-laden thermos top in one hand, a sandwich in the other, and her handbag over her shoulder, she walked several blocks to the city to shop.

And then there was the social piece as in, "Anna, come down for coffee," a clarion call from her sister who lived on the first floor. They had been talking all day but had more to say, over a cup of coffee of course. Mom dropped everything and flew down the stairs.

Or Dad's "Anna, how'd ya like to go out for coffee an'? In the Studs Lonigan novels, that meant coffee, or more likely booze, and a cigarette. But for my parents, it meant something like coffee and a treat. Rather than a doughnut, their treat was a strawberry shortcake and a coffee at the nearby Triangle Diner on a Saturday night.

What would they think of all the coffee shops today? And the prices? And the varieties? Coffee shops in my parents' day were diners where you sat at a counter and ordered one selection of coffee for ten cents.

Johann Sebastian Bach writes, in his "Coffee Cantata" from the eighteenth century. "Coffee, I have to have coffee."

To quote the authors of the NEJM article, "Current evidence does not warrant recommending caffeine or coffee intake for disease prevention but suggests that for adults who … do not have specific health conditions, moderate consumption of coffee … can be part of a healthy lifestyle."

The average coffee consumption in America is less than two cups per day. Moderate consumption? Not for my parents. Coffee was their ambrosia, a necessary, daily, work, and social ritual; the number of cups be dammed.

Dad died at 84, Mom at 93.

Who Purged My Comic Books?

In writing last week about how painful it was for me to jettison books, I was reminded of what happened to my comic books some years ago. I was also reminded of Michael Chabon's Pulitzer Prize-winning novel, one of my favorites, *The Amazing Adventures of Kavalier & Clay*.

In the novel, Kavalier and Clay become major figures in the comics industry from its nascency into its Golden Age. It is a stunning novel in which the poignant adventures of two young prodigies reveal much of what happened to America in the mid-twentieth century. The novel's heroes collaborate to create the supermen, stories, and art for one of America's greatest and well-loved novelties: the comic book. It is an amazing walk through the comic book industry, and I loved every bit of it. Yes, I have read the book twice and now, with memories of it tweaked, I will read it again.

In the 1950s, my friends and I caught the comic book frenzy. We bought and swapped but being possessive, I stopped buying and trading because the eighty-six I owned became so personal.

I kept them in a safe place: the bottom drawer of the large bureau in my bedroom, just under Dad's pristine copy of the *Providence Journal's* 1938 Hurricane issue.

The books were an entertaining escape. The stories were plain good; believable conflicts with good and bad guys, just like in the movies. I read them repeatedly, submersing my latest read to the bottom of the pile. It took weeks to read the cycle. When I returned to the first the comic was refreshed.

My eighty-six comics were a big-league collection with an all-star cast: Superman, Captain Marvel, Green Lantern, Batman, Tarzan, Plastic Man, Wonder Woman, and my cowboys, Roy, and Gene. Because I had seen Roy and Gene live at the R.I. Arena, their books became even more personal.

I read about Donald Duck and his mischievous nephews, Huey,

Dewey, and Louie. Nancy, Sluggo, Archie, Mary Jane, and Sniffles were in the pile. I had a warm spot for Archie and his friends because they hung out at a soda shop much like the one my friends and I visited after the Friday night movies.

I owned a few of the Classics Illustrated. *Ivanhoe, The Count of Monte Cristo,* and *The Three Musketeers* gave me some comfort that these comics were literature. They were Classics. They absolved me of some guilt of not reading the real thing, and I could say, "Yes" when the teachers asked me if I had read any of them during summer break.

The comics had their cheerful and sad moments.

Cheerful, because they were plain fun. Good guys defeating the enemy, teenage stars, daredevils taking chances, and heroes always winning. As I became absorbed with their escapades, they made me feel good.

Sad, because one day they were gone, vanished. I am not sure what happened to them. Maybe Dad threw them out in a purge. I could have cried.

I did.

CHAPTER IV

GRANDPARENTS, IMMIGRATION

Why Did They Settle in Rhode Island?

My courageous grandparents came to America in the early 1900s because they were poor and starving in Italy. They believed that here they would have a chance to escape poverty, find a job, build a home, and bring up children. That was not likely to happen in the old country.

They landed here because of a social principle called chain migration; not a new term by any means. Friends and relatives wrote to them, "Come to this place (R.I.) in America where you can speak the same language (regional dialect) and be understood. The stores carry the same things as in our village. People will help." All four of my grandparents made Federal Hill their first stop but hardly the last.

Chain migration is the social process by which migrants from towns follow others from that same area to a specific destination. Prospective immigrants learn of opportunities, are given prospects for accommodations and employment arranged by those who preceded them. It was a link, a bond, a social chain.

It's nothing new. The dynamic is so simple and common sense: people are more likely to move to where those they know live, and each new immigrant, in turn, makes people they know more likely to move there; a convenient circle.

Germans fleeing chaos in Europe in the mid-1800s, Irish fleeing famine in Ireland in the same years, Eastern European Jews who emigrated from the Russian and Austro-Hungarian Empires in the late 1800s and early 1900s. Italians and Japanese, escaping poverty and seeking healthier economic conditions in the same period, joined the journey. The French to Woonsocket. The Azoreans and Portuguese to comfortable neighborhoods in Rhode Island.

Immigrants came in their prime working years, survived, and made enormous economic contributions to the United States. Employers wanted them. They felt welcomed. Resulting "colonies" from the same villages, towns, and cities settled in Boston, New York, Buenos Aires, Toronto, Montreal, Sydney, etc. from the mid-1800s through the mid-1900s. An example: the Czechs, attracted by employment and an opportunity to buy land, went to Nebraska in the late nineteenth century. Germans for similar reasons trekked to the Great Plains. Again, nothing new.

Ethnic enclaves, like those on Federal Hill, a site first settled by the Irish, were built and sustained by immigrants. Different ethnic groups claimed distinct spaces in city neighborhoods, provided a welcome, and maintained the community network. Ties to that community remained particularly strong with first-generation immigrants. Eventually, they moved on to something better.

My grandparents, like all those immigrants, loved this country and embraced everything about it. They worked, raised families, joined community organizations, churches, made economic contributions, built homes, and most importantly, guaranteed that their children and grandchildren would get an education. They created opportunities for us, and we capitalized on the chances readily available in this great country.

Thank you, grandparents. Thank you for the chance. If you only knew today how much you have given us.

My Grandfather's Diaries

This is the first of a series of grandfather articles. No worries. When I finish these, there will be a Grandma article or two.

Some years ago, Diane found my grandfather's diaries tucked on a shelf under the stairs in the basement of my parents' home. The wrinkled, dusty covers of black fading to gray chronicled the years from 1938 to 1941 in recessed gold numbers. Thought lost or not thought of at all, they had not been opened for years, from the day he died in 1952.

As we were rummaging, Diane stopped, "Look at these." I was surprised when she handed them to me.

Until that day, I had thought little of his background. The diaries gave me the incentive to search. In Italian and with poor handwriting, nonetheless, there were parts I understood. Most of what he wrote was of his day's wages, never more than a dollar. He wrote of births and deaths. In one graphic entry of December 1939, he wrote, "I believe there will be another world war." Imagine. He wrote it two years before the United States entered the war.

For the first time, I began to think of where in Italy he was from, why he emigrated, what he did in Italy, how he was prescient about the war. I was surprised to learn that though he was literate of the Italian language, fifty percent of the immigrants were not. Imagine coming to America unable to read or write your own language and now having to learn a new one. How did he cope with the new language?

How did he read a document, a bill, learn complex words, and express himself when he wanted something ... directions, bank statements, citizenship papers? How did he keep an appointment or ask for a promotion? Was he offered one? How might he know?

How did he handle the indignity of his new illiteracy?

What did he do when people made fun of his dress? His accent?

Finding those diaries make me think. What do you keep when your parents die? What do you keep of your grandparents that your parents kept? And now, as we begin to think of downsizing, it gives me pause. What do we take? Leave behind? To whom? What does it matter?

In my early years I enjoyed being around my grandfather, watching him work in his garden, building a shed, planting his vegetables, tending his fruit trees, burying the fig tree for the winter.

Since I have had his diaries, I have wanted to know more of this gentle, quiet, hard-working family man. I would like to see his face again, to look into his caring eyes and ask him some questions.

When I give presentations, I show pictures of those diaries along with a picture of his passport. They are stark reminders of his path from Italy to American citizenship through education and hard work. And I delight in the nostalgia I rekindle in my audiences.

Grandpa's diaries fit nicely in my drawer.

A Grandfather's Courage

I wish I had known my Dad's father better or, for that matter, at all. My Dad and his siblings spoke of their difficult childhood. Their Mom died at the birth of her seventh child, who also passed. Needing to work while requiring help with his children, my grandfather had his recently married cousins move in with him and his family. The cousins eventually had seven children of their own: both families living together for a while. Three adults and thirteen kids lived in a small four-room flat. In time, the cousins moved further down the street to their own place.

The thirteen children grew close, becoming more like brothers and sisters. As soon as they were able, they went to work, some as young as fourteen (our Dad one of them).

Our grandfather, aunts, and uncles lived in a small tenement on Tell Street in the Federal Hill section of Providence. The tenement, one of six in a bulky building, stood within touching distance of another behemoth of the same size across a narrow alley. It was a second-floor walk-up, the door opening directly into the kitchen from the hallway. Three small rooms (two bedrooms, a den) and a small pantry were off the kitchen.

In the early years, my aunt Vera, the oldest at thirteen, stayed home from school to raise her siblings. When the truant officer came, she hid.

My grandfather, Carmine, was mostly a shadow in my mind. Because he was not well and spoke only Italian, I did not have a chance to chat with him, nor did I do things with him as I did with my mother's father who lived with us in our house a neighborhood away. We were told of Carmine's courage, one which came in quiet doses. It took years before I appreciated his, and my aunt Vera's.

Dad stayed connected to his boyhood home. Two of his sisters and his father lived there for some years after Dad married. His visit was a Sunday ritual ... church, visit with family and then meet his longtime friends at the corner drug store on Broadway. I was fortunate to trail along.

On some Sundays, after visiting with my aunts, we went to visit with the cousins, some of whom still lived in their small tenement. They were so delighted to see us. In all the years of visiting, I never heard a malicious thought, self-pity, or jealousy of those more fortunate. They worked hard to fulfill their needs, doing what was necessary, working to survive and appreciating what they had. They were grateful to their parents and this country for giving them that opportunity.

I loved those Sunday mornings. As I look back on them today, it helps me recognize and appreciate the courage of our immigrant grandparents and their offspring. Like so many others of their generation, they gave us our opportunities. They taught us, by example, about the importance of family and perseverance.

How fortunate we were.

Why Didn't They Smile?

During my presentations, I show several old pictures of my immigrant grandparents and relatives in their later years in Italy and early days in America. One thing conspicuous in the pictures is that they did not smile. It is the rare image where a twinkle, even a slight crack at the side of the mouth, is visible. No, they do not look uncomfortable. Rather, they look proper, sitting upright or standing tall; a formality that conveys a twinge of sadness. If that were the case, there would be good reasons.

Life was difficult in the old country and, love their land or not, to survive they were forced to relocate. To book passage, come across the ocean under duress, land in a place where they did not speak the language and had no place to live or work, was daunting.

My memories of growing up among them are not what one sees in the photos. Rather, I remember the pleased, proud, and laughing group of my childhood; gathering with pride to eat, drink, play music, dance, and sing. The fears of relocation and survival were dwindling, the constraint of hardship in the mirror. I ask the audience when I project the picture, "Is there anything you notice?"

After a slight pause, they respond, "Yes. They're not smiling."

"Right. Why do you think that is?"

The responses are thoughtful and sometimes amusing. "They weren't happy? Things were tough in those early days. They were sitting too long because photography was slow, and shutters did not snap quickly enough." I like this one. "They had bad teeth."

"Those are good ideas, but no, that was not the case. Any others?"

"Superstition? If they smiled, it meant that things were good. And, if so, they feared that subsequent days would bring something not so good, even bad. Misfortune might arise tomorrow if they were happy today." Not a bad response.

For example, when one asks an Italian how he is, he usually says, "Non c'e' male" or "Cosi cosi … not so bad, so-so." To say, "Very good" might bring bad luck. A smile might do the same.

No, neither is that the answer.

The explanation I heard from an elder Italian made sense. "They did not smile because it was just not something they did. They believed it did not look good. They were happy enough, but their culture dictated that it was inappropriate to smile in a photo, as a smile might reflect poor behavior, a poor presence. Italians are quite conscious of their behavior in public." This was an explanation that made the most sense. It was cultural.

Pictures from later years show families established, educated, prosperous and enmeshed in a new culture in America, away from the chaos of the old country. In this setting, people smiled. The old-timers still fought it a bit, but Mom, Dad, aunts, uncles, and cousins did not.

They were happy. They were established in America.

They Had Their Sayings

With the onset of the COVID epidemic, a new lexicon has flooded our ears … don the mask, curb the virus, social distancing, herd immunity, I'll see you on Zoom, we must flatten the curve.

In my youth, the polio epidemic generated phrases … iron lung, infantile paralysis, get a shot and Salk vaccine.

These colloquialisms further reminded me of bygone days when my father, mother, relatives, and friends had their favorite sayings, some lingering to this day. At family gatherings, we rekindle them, laughing over the oft-repeated quips as if they just happened.

My uncles had a few that have made their way into family history, such as 'New York Jints (Giants)' and hockey 'gooley' (goalie). There was also "Hit it with the hose," if Uncle Carlo wanted to rinse the soap from the car. When speaking of singer Rosemary Clooney, one uncle said, "She's married to Joe Ferrara." He meant, of course, Jose Ferrer. Or he used Calvin instead of Kevin when summoning my nephew. From another uncle: "He ain't got it," for a lousy ballplayer.

From our dear friend when she overheard a conversation about her niece who was planning to become a veterinarian. "Whaddya mean? She eats meat!"

My parents' phrases are those most recounted by our children and nephews.

Picture this scene: As my parents are chugging along, Dad driving, Mom window shopping, some poor soul inadvertently cut them off. Dad, blurts, "That guy's a menace." Mom: "Peter, maybe he has a condition." Dad: "Condition, hell. He's a hindrance!"

Some of Dad's favorites: When we went to a restaurant, he was quick to reach into his wallet, even before the dinner was served, turn to me and bark, "What do I owe ya?"

"Take care of a car and it will take care of you." "I'll send you the hell home," when our kids were misbehaving. "I din getcha," as his hearing diminished in later years.

More from Dad. As winter approached: "We lost an hour." After the solstice: "The days get longer by a minute each day." And I am sure you are not surprised to hear that he said it every day.

Mom had her share: "Why, no good?" when she served a delicious dish and you asked where she bought the products or what her recipe was. "It's in the fridge," when the kids were looking for a snack. When picking candy from her pocketbook, she turned, brightened, and offered it to her grandchildren with, "Here's a little goodie. How can you say no to candy?"

Or her admonishment about eating too much, "Don't get a belly."

When she did not approve of someone's garb: "She dresses like Astor's pet horse." Where that came from is anybody's guess. "He has nice ears," when she met her granddaughter's fiancé.

Or the universal one that I heard in so many homes … "Eat! Eat! I don't mind you eating, but don't throw it away."

Share some of yours.

CHAPTER V

HOLIDAYS

Magical Memories of the Holiday Season

We met a dear friend after the wonderful Messiah concert on Saturday night at the Vets. Richard found us in the exiting crowd to wish us a joyful season, but more so to give me a recent newspaper clipping of the story of how his Dad made a generous wooden Christmas sleigh complete with Santa and reindeer some sixty years ago.

I remember that sleigh because Dick's brother, Joe, was my treasured partner in the practice of medicine for many years. When their Dad died, Joe was the first to inherit the sleigh and proudly displayed it on his lawn as did his Dad. When Joe died, Dick inherited the prize and is now restoring it to its storied glory for his display. Tradition, love, and memories. That's what defines the holidays. And thus, my memories.

The advent of the holiday season transports me to days of joy, excitement, and family. Songs of Christmas filled the airwaves, announcing the start of the season, and decorations popped up magically in stores and homes. Ornamental lights, wreaths, trees, and nativity scenes were set. Anticipation and excitement filled the air.

It was a tradition for Mom to take me to downtown Providence. As we left the bus at LaSalle Square, we walked by the Majestic Theater and the City Hall Hardware Store where there was a toy department. Toys were spinning in my head. She pulled me from store to store, entering and exchanging the commotion of the city – cars, buses, walkers, and talkers – for the softer sounds of the stores with the smells of wood and pine. We passed Gladding's, Kennedys, Shepard's to Woolworth's, cutting through Pie Alley, stopping to look, maybe to buy, Mom never letting go of my hand.

The town was bubbling with people, sounds, tinsel, and bells. I have watched *The Christmas Story* movie many times. When Ralphie's family journeys to downtown Hohman, Indiana, I am reminded of some of the same treasures we lined up to see at the Outlet store window displays … toys, trains, dolls, sleds, and Santa's animated string-puppet elves. Waves of people strolled the streets, admiring the windows and stopping to chat, sharing their day. "What did you buy?" "Very nice." "Have you eaten?" "Where?" "Coffee?"

And then into the store and up the stairs to find Santa and the grab bag where a treasure awaited. Our Santa, unlike Ralphie's, was caring and convincing.

Before leaving the city, Mom was sure to take me to the Boston Store where I devoured the best custard pie and glass of milk ever. We then made our way to the bus stop where across the street was the Hong Hong Restaurant, its steamy aromas, and mystery of fortune cookies filling the air. Mom ordered our evening meal and toted it, along with her other bags, home on the bus.

I was tired, full enough of downtown with its sounds and spaces. But I felt so good, happy, so excited.

Doings on the 4th

If there were one day of the year that I could recreate, it would be the Fourth of July of my youth.

Weeks out of school and a long way from the history lessons of founding fathers, we had almost forgotten the reasons for the celebration – but not the best part! Living in the city meant a bonfire. With the crackle of salutes and the pop of Roman candles echoing through the neighborhood, the biggest challenge of July 4th was to build the biggest bonfire. "We'll light it in the middle of the intersection."

We stored our wood supplies under the cover of bushes, porches, and rear yards. As darkness crept in, kids carried their wood to the pile, making half turns, winding out a throw to the top like a discus toss, piling wood as high as the first-floor level of a tenement house. Someone ran from the shadows, splashing liquid that smelled like the Shell station on the pile. A match and whoosh, the boom and crackles of the fire blew.

The neighborhood, once lit by dim streetlights, was now alive with a dancing glow of yellows, reds, greens, and the smell of dense smoke. Shadows that covered trees and houses disappeared. Flames danced in the windows. Thinking the neighbors would be happy with the celebration, we were stunned to hear "Damn kids! Call the cops! Get the fire department before we all go up in flames!"

Later, in bed, but too excited to sleep, I lay awake listening to the booms of cherry bombs exploding.

Some summers, we rented a cottage on the Narragansett shore where we went to the outdoor movies on Saturday nights. Bearing blankets, sweatshirts, hats, long khaki pants, Citronella Oil, and an Army flashlight hooked to my belt, we strolled to a nearby store where in the lot was a white wooden screen attached to a four-foot post bearing a cone-shaped speaker. Propped on a nearby table was a two-reel projector with its wire running along the lot to and through a barely open store window.

The soft light bathing the parking lot and the one flowing from the projector attracted swarms of moths and an occasional June bug. A buzz tickled my ears. I felt a nip on my hand. I slapped. Splat. Blood! Mosquitoes! Platoons arising from the camouflage of the nearby marsh swarmed like enemy bombers.

With the speed of a gunslinger, I whipped out the Citronella and spread its yellow oil on my face (ugh) neck and arms. The stink was sickening, but not for the mosquitoes. They loved it. They dove to dine.

A welcoming breeze from the ocean carried a salty dew to my face. My sun-warmed skin was cold. Goosebumps blended with bites. I yearned for my warm bed. The movie ended. Floodlights lit. Folding chairs snapped. Car engines started. The fog lifted. The horn stopped. It was time to go.

We started our walk to the cabin accompanied by fireflies under a cloudless sky with a full moon, brilliant stars, and waves crashing in the distance as I thought of bonfires, fireworks, and outdoor movies.

I love the Fourth of July. It means summer.

My Italo-Turkey Day

I know many of you have seen this before, but because it rekindles memories, be you of Italian roots or not, I thought I might publish it at least one more time; first time here on GoLocal. For those who have read it before, thank you. For those who have not, please take a moment to reflect on your Family Day and what it means to you.

Dad said, "They don't have turkey in Italy." I wasn't sure what he meant. It was Thanksgiving, there was a high-school football game, a chill in the air and our family was about to have a feast. The only differences between this day and the usual Sunday dinner were that we ate turkey rather than chicken, there was cranberry sauce, and it was Thursday.

My grandparents knew nothing of Thanksgiving when they arrived in America. "But they found a way," my aunt said. "My mother was progressive. She learned how to stuff a turkey. She learned about yams and cranberries." The grandparents were assimilating, more so now that the war was over, and they were no longer considered enemy aliens.

Grandmother never saw a turkey before arriving here from Pollutri, a small town in Abruzzo, Italy. She knew nothing of Pilgrims and how they celebrated their good fortunes in America. She was comforted, however, when she learned that she shared something with those early settlers; they also arrived in fear, ignorance, expectation, and hope. Perhaps she felt this bond. She became more involved, more American. Thus, she learned how to cook a turkey dinner for Thanksgiving not because she had to, but because she wanted to. And she was becoming more proficient in English for the same reason. She wanted to. She was American.

I returned from the football game to the wonderful aromas infusing the rear staircase of our Providence three family tenement home. Our families sat around a huge table. The warm light streaming through the dining room windows brought something magic that made every Sunday and every holiday dinner beautiful. The children had their own table in the adjoining parlor, just as splendid as the adults' table. The feast began after a thankful prayer. Antipasto first, followed by lasagna and hot dumpling soup. The turkey, carried by grandfather, was presented as King.

Mashed potatoes, turnips, sweet potatoes, and cranberry sauce accompanied. Grandfather scooped out the stuffing, carved and served the turkey. We ladled out brown, not Italian red, gravy. When finished, we thought that we neither could nor would, eat another thing.

Oh, those desserts; pumpkin, apple, and custard pies, torrone, spumoni, confetti (candy almonds), biscotti, noce (nuts), mandorle (almonds), nocciole (hazelnuts) and gelato. Stovetop-roasted chestnuts followed. Coke and Nehi sodas and grandfather's homemade wine washed everything down.

My grandparents did what people in America have always done for Thanksgiving. They appreciated and embraced it and added their culture. They taught us that it was our holiday, our American holiday, new and now familiar. It may have been "Italianized," but it was now clearly American.

Downtown with Mom at Christmas

My excitement grew as we walked from our home on Wealth Avenue to the bus stop on Academy Avenue. Mom was taking me to downtown Providence. It was Christmas, and I was as excited as the first time that Dad took me to Fenway Park to see The Red Sox.

I stood on the curb, leaning, watching, and waiting. The bus arrived with a screeching hiss; its doors whisked open. I bounded on and sat with my forehead and nose pressed against the cold glass, drawing a Santa in the steam. The bus swung around the corner onto Atwells Avenue and climbed Federal Hill, stuttering to several stops along the way.

We left the bus at LaSalle Square, walked by the Majestic Theater, the White Tower, and the City Hall Hardware Store where there was a toy department. My feet were dancing, toys spinning in my head. "Later, Edward."

Tides of people strolled through the streets with a purpose, admiring the windows and stopping to chat, sharing their day. "What did you buy?" "Very nice." "Have you eaten?" "Where?" "Coffee?"

I shifted as they spoke of dresses and shoes. "C'mon, Mom." I tugged. She pulled me from store to store, exchanging the commotion of the city – cars, busses, walkers, and talkers – for the muted sounds from the stores, the smell of clothes, wood, and the pine of Christmas decorations.

For eleven months of the year, the stores' windows changed regularly with new fashions and seasonal displays. This was different. It was Christmas stuff, and I was thrilled.

We passed Gladdings, Kennedys, Shepherds (meet you under the clock) to Woolworth's, cutting through Pie Alley, stopping to look, maybe to buy, Mom never letting go of my hand. Finally, we arrived at The Outlet store.

The windows were alive with Christmas ... toys, clothes, dolls, Santa, stirring puppets, a whirling train, and animated elves. Inside was my visit with Santa (I had been to the toy department, so I knew what I wanted). From the grab bag, I plucked a bag of goodies, one of them a Chinese finger trap.

At the end of our Saturday, before heading home, we made our way to the Hon Hong Restaurant where steamy aromas filled the air, and the mystery of fortune cookies filled my mind. Mom ordered our evening meal and toted it, along with her other bags, home on the bus.

As we passed Federal Hill, I saw the beginnings of the late afternoon ritual of people streaming out of their homes to stroll, talk and to buy. The pushcarts were out. Red and green lights filled the air. "Here Comes Santa Claus" was playing in the background.

I was tired, full enough of downtown with its noises and distances, and I was hungry. But I felt so good, so happy, so eager.

More than window displays, Santa, the grab bag, smells, and decorations, there were people. That's what made it fun. That's what made Christmas. It was the people.

Downtown Providence at Christmas was the place.

Dad's Christmas Tree

This is one of my annual Christmas stories. I hope it will rekindle your memories of family and holidays.

Dad would arrive home one evening before Christmas

with the tree tied to the roof of his car.

He carried it in, secured it in the stand, and positioned it by the largest window. He strung the lights in a spiral, hung the ornaments, draped the tinsel, stuck the star on the top, and stood back. Perfect. Dad decorated a Christmas tree the way he did everything else, with pride.

No, it was not the best or the most adorned, and it would not win any prizes. But it was one of a kind ... his.

My first memory was of the blur of lights, a glow that filled the corners of my eyes with mist. His tree was as green as a summer day and smelled as fresh as forest evergreens.

It collected streams of winter light that bounced off the ornaments and the tinsel, filtering through the branches to the walls and the carpet. Motes drifted in the living room's air.

In the heart of the tree was Dad's favorite ornament, Santa. "I bought that Santa when you were born."

Made of cloth, stitched, and glued, he was no more than four inches high, wore a tall red hat with a white cotton rim, a long red jacket that hung to his knees, light blue pants, a tan sack over his left shoulder and black boots. His droopy, pink face and blue eyes seemed to sing with the season's joy.

Year after year Dad hung his Santa. I married and had children. On Christmas Day, Dad strolled to his tree, pointed, and smiled, "That Santa is as old as your father."

Over the years Santa aged; his beard turned from white to tan, he lost his left hand, his pants drooped, pine needles stuck to his boots, his sack shriveled, the piping on the front of his jacket needed stitching, the cotton withered. But his joy continued.

My Dad died in 1996. We bought a small tree for Mom and decorated it, never failing to place the Santa. Mom died six years later. As we discarded the old decorations, I panicked. Where was Santa? At the last moment, I spotted him, surrounded by hunks of tinsel, attached to Mom's tree. I snatched him. He now took his place on my tree. "See that Santa. Pop bought it when I was born."

One year, I misplaced the Santa. In a panic, I searched everywhere to no avail and Santa missed Christmas for the first time. The following year I found him, lying in the bottom of a box of ornaments, smiling, or maybe smirking. I took a deep breath as memories resurfaced and melted to tears. "I found him! I found him!"

Santa returned to the heart of our tree. As our grandchildren arrive on Christmas Day, I direct them to the tree. "See that Santa. My Dad bought him when I was born."

Dad's tree will ever remain one of a kind … ours.

Blindsided at Thanksgiving

There is a certain cadence to a Thanksgiving Day, and it was lost this year. When I was a kid, the day began with a football game played in the unfriendly cold. I attended games with friends, sometimes with Dad, in later years with my children. While be-bopping in the stands to keep warm, my body may have listened, but my toes did not. Rock hard, frozen digits did not seem worth the effort, as there was never enough hot chocolate at the concession stand to turn the thermal current to uncomfortable tapping toes. Sure, I drank plenty, but it dictated trips to the ice-locker, men's room, no better.

I then substituted outdoor football with the indoors of Macy's Day balloons on TV, but that wore thin.

So here we are this year, now some days after Thanksgiving. Falling leaves, bouncing cheerleaders, ducking the cold before turkey dinner did not define the day. Nor did the family gathering. We were blindsided.

In the past, Diane and I were fortunate to have two Thanksgivings … one on Wednesday evening at our daughter's in Hingham where we had anything but turkey … Chinese, Mexican, Thai or whatever.

And the following day at our daughter's in East Greenwich where tradition reigned. Well, not the tradition of the cold toes. We skipped alternative morning festivities to drive directly for hugs and food.

This year, Diane and I dined alone, a candle here, music there, a little Prosecco and the traditional dinner warmth with a hitch. There still was the comfort of the toasty, brown aroma of the turkey dinner floating above, but there was a touch of sadness in the unusual, palpable calm, a void in the jovial holiday scene. The thread of conversation of who likes white or dark meat, the sit back, "I'm bloated" blurt as we looked at arriving pies, was not there.

However, the spirit lingered as we did not fail to reflect on what made us thankful, though it was less easy in this not so ordinary time; not when the pandemic has taken so much from so many.

Though it was an unconventional Thanksgiving Day, Diane and I took a moment to reflect on those who have lost so much, those who have had a monumental struggle. And to pray for them.

I am thankful that I will be able to move forward into December when, after the solstice, each day grows longer by a minute, when the virus' beat will retreat, when the vaccine is introduced, when we can begin to return to normal, howsoever it may be.

I love the last stanza of Mary Oliver's poem, "Messenger."

> ... which is gratitude, to be given a mind and a heart
> and these body-clothes,
> a mouth with which to give shouts of joy
> to the moth and the wren, to the sleepy dug-up clam,
> telling them all, over and over, how it is
> that we live forever.

Yes, indeed.

CHAPTER VI

TIME

How Old Do You Feel?

I thought of my advancing age not long ago when I re-read Roger Angell's' marvelous essay, "This Old Man" in the February 2014 issue of *The New Yorker*. In his nineties, he writes of prominent knuckles, blurred vision, shooting pains, and health issues, but within that litany, he stated, "I'm ninety-three, and I'm feeling great."

I'm not going to disclose my age because as a friend once said, "When I look out, I feel thirty-five." Well, though I don't quite feel thirty-five, I have an edgy feeling that I can do everything I did when I was thirty-five. It's an uneasy feeling, because when I look in the mirror while shaving, I see my father. When my father was fifty, I thought he was old, probably because, in those days, he was.

Some years ago, I wrote of having hands like my grandfather's. Not those heavy, gnarly and calloused of a working man, but soft and smooth; a reflection of a lifetime in one school or another. The dorsal sides reveal prominent veins, spots, and wrinkles that have crept into what once were unblemished mitts. They bruise easily and the bruises turn brown and linger. My knuckles seem bigger, but except for a small knob on the farthest digit of my second finger where I choke the pen to write (yes, I still write with a pen), I have no calluses. Nevertheless, at least on the backs, I have hands like Papa's, not gnarled or crooked, just aged from exposure to the sun.

I take a few pills, one prescription, and some vitamins. My knees twinge a bit after a round of golf; probably because I carry my bag. I have a resilient ego and pretend I can do it with ease. My lower spine needs oil, so I try to loosen it with the groans of a morning stretch, thinking it will help me to hit the golf ball just as I did when I was younger, err … thirty-five that is.

Save for occasional premature beats, my heart behaves, plodding along in marching rhythm. I was once working alone in the gym, using the overhead lift, thinking I nailed it with consecutive reps. Two young men strolled by on their way to the locker room, one muttering to the other, "Gee, the old guy's in pretty good shape." I looked around. I was the only one in the gym. I was the 'old guy'!

I can handle it. I look for the senior citizen discount. I go for the early bird specials. I enjoy a good joke and ply my writing pen with enthusiasm. I have become mellow with memories.

It's OK. I realize I am lucky and appreciate it. I can take the aches. I can take those who call me "Sir." I turn up the TV. But … I ain't quittin'.

Though I've been lucky with my health, one never knows when the sword of Damocles might fall.

I like looking out.

Trying to Understand Time

I received quite several responses following my last article about the aging process. As I think about it, I am trying to understand the concept of time. Not so easy. Coincidentally, I recently read a National Geographic article which suggests that "to be human is to migrate through time." Well, what do they mean?

Does time really flow? When I try to think of it with physics or space, my mind freezes. I cannot seem to grasp the concepts that Einstein did so easily. (Well, he was *the* genius). As I write, every stroke of the pen suggests that time is passing from one word to the next. Can you feel it as you work, play, read, etc.?

Time controls me. I have a deadline to submit an article every week. The week flies. In my career, I was early to the hospital and early for every meeting. I never could help being neurotic. A banker once said to me, "If you want the winter to pass quickly, take out a ninety-day note." Yep, that concept I understand.

Einstein's insights from special relativity provide evidence that time does not flow. There he goes again. I don't get that. I read as much as I can, I think about it often, but I cannot grasp Einstein's theories. So, I hark back to an article I wrote some years ago about what time and "a time" meant to Italian families. Time was something different, understood though almost indefinable. Here's a common conversation:

"In school they told us drinking is bad. Do you drink, Dad?"

"Drink? Me? Noooo. Well, I might have a beer if I'm at a 'Time.'"

"A 'Time?'" What's that?"

"You know. Where lots of people get together ... eat, drink, talk about you, hug and kiss you and give you gifts. Now you can say they gave you a 'Time.' And they say, "What a 'Time' it was!" Now, do you understand?" "Nope."

"Try this. A 'Time' is what happens after someone graduates, has an anniversary, or gets married."

"Oh. Now I think I understand. People come for you. They dress up, eat, drink, talk around and sometimes they're just there."

"Yeah, and they leave a gift like a Cross pen and pencil set. Or rosary beads."

"Yeah, I like that. So, you can have a 'Time' at any time, right?"

"Well almost, but not really. You have to do something, like receive your First Communion, or die."

"OK. And the 'Time' is at a special time of day, right?"

"Right."

And the timing for the 'Time' must be timed for you and what you did, right?"

"Right."

And you just can't have a 'Time' any old time, right?"

"Right. Now you get it."

"Yep, now I get it. I'm getting dressed. Let's go to a 'Time.'"

"Your timing is perfect."

"Thanks, Dad. Wait. One other thing. I'll bet they gave Einstein quite a 'Time' when he discovered that stuff about time."

"Right again."

"Then let's go. We're off to a 'Time.'"

Time on Ellis Island

When I give presentations, there is an emotional point I reach and for which I need to take a deep breath to continue. It happens when I speak of family, particularly the heroism of my grandparents and their arrival to America.

Their courage was undaunted. I experienced that courage (to a small degree) and was filled with emotion when I visited Ellis Island and the Statue of Liberty last weekend.

As we left Battery Park in Manhattan on the ferry to the Statue, there was a moment when I was able to glimpse her through the window of the boat. I backed away from the window, trying to experience a look that one might have when seeing her through the porthole of a ship, just as my grandparents might when they arrived here in the early 1900s from Italy. Imagine how they felt. Imagine the emotions that welled in their chests ... anxiety, excitement, pride, hope, and utter fright. Tears welled as I tried to feel their courage and fears. Sitting nearby was a young mother pointing out Lady Liberty to her children. I could not help but mention, "The statue is the first thing my grandparents saw when they arrived in America."

"Really?" I took pride in explaining where they came from and why, finishing by saying, "When you get to the Statue, look for the poem by Emma Lazarus at its base. Part of it says, 'Give me your tired, your poor, your huddled masses yearning to breathe free.' My grandparents were among those yearning masses."

I appreciated her echo. "Really?"

After visiting the Statue, we took the ferry to Ellis Island; another emotional bolt as Diane and I stood speechless picturing our grandparents surviving the tests to make it through. I will write more of the Island in another piece, but there is another observation that to me was so important. Of the hundreds and hundreds of people who traveled on these ferries and visited these sites along with us last week, many were newer arrivals to America. They were eager to see Ellis Island and, from the variety of languages I heard, my guess is that, although they were much younger than we, their enthusiasm was just as current.

I heard little English. I heard no Italian. Rather, I heard a remarkable panoply of languages ... different tones, rhythms, inflections, speeds ... all of which I wished I could speak because of the beauty and rhythm of the spoken song.

I was pleased that they were visiting these National Parks to learn of the roots of this great country. I was pleased to see them pointing out the monuments while telling the stories to their children. I suspect none of them had ancestors that came through the Island. I realized then that I was looking at tomorrow while reflecting upon yesterday, and with that look forward, I saw what immigrants of one hundred years ago, my grandparents among them, did for us and for this country.

Yes, it was an emotional day.

Can I Go Backward in Time?

I cannot seem to get off this business of time, probably because I wanted to travel back in that dimension when I went to Ellis Island recently. I was trying to grasp, picture, what was happening when my grandparents arrived. No, not what was happening in history, but what was going on with them as they looked to the future. I wanted to find a way to be there. Of course, I could not.

Time travel means moving forward, or backward (really?), to different points in time, much like you might move between different points in space. Physicists define time as the progression of events from the past to present into the future. If a system is unchanging, it is timeless. OK. Time is not something we can see, touch, or taste, but we can measure its passage. I think I understand that. However, as I reflect on my grandparents' experiences, I realize I can only measure those events in my memory.

I appreciate that time is temporary and irreversible. What I want to do is grasp it, grasp the past, and put myself there so I can fathom further what those immigrants felt. How do I travel back? Forget the physicists, psychologists, and space scientists. I've read enough of their 'takes' on time. I recognize that the key is merely in my mind.

For example, time seems to speed up as we get older. Psychologists have shown that adults perceive time as moving faster than it did when they were children. I didn't need a psychologist to tell me that. I could have told them. Forget speed. I want time to be so slow that is goes backward.

Most of us can equate time with places we have been. No, I am not talking about travel. I am talking about neighborhoods and events …

the home run off the house, the schoolyard where you pitched cards, the terror of walking from the movies at night. I can tell you when those things happened and where I was. Where were you when … ?

This I understand: time is the progression of events from the past into the future. For non-scientists, time moves only in one direction. It's possible to move forward in time, but not backward. When we were kids, we were carefree in wishing time away. "I wish I were old enough to drive, I can't wait to go to the movies on my own, I wish I were old enough to drink."

So, how do I travel back? With pictures, stories, memories, and imagination. What is the key? I guess it's about where I want to be. And the only way I can recreate it is with images, awareness, chats with relatives, writing and places like Ellis Island.

Imagine, more than 12 million immigrants made their first stop in America at the Ellis Island Immigration Station between 1892 and 1954, and my grandparents were among them.

I see them in the crowd.

Even the Garden Has Its Time

It was another walk-through time, one which I have done in the fall for years, through my garden on this glorious day. I picked my last zucchini before it was fully ripened. Though it had time to mature, I was concerned about an early frost hovering around the corner.

This was not just any zucchini. It was a special, three-foot-long, bulbous Italian heirloom called a *Zuchetta rampicante,* named so because in its growth, its vines ran rampant through the garden, wandering onto the fence, the trellis, around the tomato plants, anywhere and with charm. The bowed vegetable can grow up to four feet long when left to maturity.

It was even more special because the plant was given to me by my friend, Mike, who had nurtured it through the winter from a seed under the ultraviolet light on his cellar shelf. He brought it to me neatly centered in a ready-to-plant peat pot. I tucked it in the ground with care in the early spring, hoping to show him that I could grow the beauty, and I did. Rather, as a *rampicante,* it kinda did its own thing.

The last prize signaled the end of the growing season, always a bit of a sad time for me. I put away the boots, spade, rake, shovel, old clothes, and the wonderful smells that come from a garden, musty dirt, sweet roses, sugary fruits, and wet dirt. I miss the colors of zinnias, marigolds, tomatoes, purple eggplants and of course, the pea green *Zuchetta.* I miss the sounds of birds bathing in my birdbaths.

The woodchuck and the villainous possum gave me a break when they left. Woodchucks love to eat everything; possums just don't smell good. I garden along with them, having long given up my battle to discourage them from coming.

One of the more important things I don't leave in my garden are the memories. When I grew up on Wealth Avenue in Providence, I gave gardening little thought for I was too involved with sports, study, and delivering the daily newspaper. It was not until later in life that I thought of planting a garden. At that point, I was motivated.

For years, I watched my grandfather from our third-floor window as he nurtured his garden next to our three-decker house. He spent hours tilling to deliver the fruits of his labor to his family. He had a fig tree, the heralded story of my first book. He buried that tree every fall to protect it for the winter. I was intrigued as I watched, never realizing that one day I might be doing the same. Yes, I have fig trees, four of them. Maybe I planted them to preserve the link between my grandfather, my family, good times, the three-decker castle, and me.

Working in the garden is peaceful. It feels right. Picking the last zucchini, though a bit sad, is fulfilling.

Time On My Wrist

I remember the day in the fifth grade when my father gave me a wristwatch. It sported a small rectangular face and a tan wristband (maybe even leather) which I quickly learned to fasten with one hand. It was a Waltham Premier, made in nearby Massachusetts. I loved it, so much so that I rolled up my sleeves to brandish it as often as I could.

Dad showed me how to remove the back to see the inner workings. There was a tiny notch on the rear cover that I was able to pry, rather pop, open with the thin blade of my jackknife. I could watch the passage of time, studying the intricacies of wheels, springs, and spokes synchronized to perfection, oscillating at a constant rate with clockwork precision to measure the passing time. "Don't ever touch those moving wheels, Edward. You'll ruin the watch. Someone had to put them together by hand, one piece at a time."

He continued. "Be sure to wind it every day if you want it to give you the correct time." No issue for me. In those days, I was more concerned with being a watch wearer than a time teller.

Dad gave me the watch when he was given a neat Navy watch at The Naval Air Station where he worked. I knew the military recognized the value of time because I had seen many an Army movie, and I remembered the oft-heard phrase, "Be sure to synchronize watches."

Dad, my grandfathers, and the old-timers also had pocket watches which they wore on special occasions. I hoped to inherit one of those, complete with fob, one day.

My teacher walked by when I was writing with pen and ink, steadying my paper at the top left with my left hand, err rather, my watch hand, sleeve rolled up. "That's a beautiful watch, Edward. Where did you get it?'

"My father gave it to me," I replied, calmly elevating my arm to rest on my elbow or scratching the back of my head so everyone could see the gleaming beauty.

I learned how to tell time. I assume I started young with first understanding the difference between PM and AM as in, "Five PM, bath time, Edward," Mom announced on a Saturday night. On Sunday, "Get up, Edward. It's eight AM, time for church," or "Be home by five-thirty for supper."

Today, I feel naked and unadorned without a wristwatch. When I look at it, I feel a sense of comfort, not only because I have ready access to time right there on my wrist, but also because I can remember that my father trusted me with the Waltham so many years ago.
It was my best mechanical friend.

I never had to change the Waltham's battery. There was none.
I was able to control time for the first and maybe only time, stopping the watch by not winding it.

If I stop my watch today, will I go back in time? Certainly. Well …

Are Friendships Governed by the Passage of Time?

Friendships are among the more important things in a lifetime. Heeding the advice of a friend, I try to call a friend every day. Philosophers have discussed what it means to be a friend. In his Nicomachean Ethics, Aristotle addresses major questions regarding friendship, believing that friends who give to each other with no expectations in return possess one of the ingredients that make for friendship and … happiness.

Though Aristotle professed that a good man does not need friends, he is clear in pointing out that a good man "cannot live a pleasant life in solitary." Aristotle thought of friendship as a necessity, claiming that we need friends in time of misfortune … friends helping to guide the young from error and the old in their weaknesses. Friends help us behave in a positive, honorable manner. Not to dwell further on what has been written so often by so many, my definition of friendship is easy; someone with whom I like to spend time.

I do not have old friends but longtime friends. I dismissed the word "old" because when we meet, I see vitality, inquisitive minds, freshness in thoughts, and reflections upon past and current endeavors.

I regularly enjoy lunches and breakfasts with longtime friends ... neighborhood, junior high school, high school, physicians, and "new" neighborhood. James Marcus would call us genetic ambassadors. I look forward to these collations with enthusiasm and respect; enthusiasm because it is plain entertaining, respect because I learn something every time we meet.

These meetings are also a measure of the passing of time as we appreciate new understandings of infirmities, fuzzy thinking, sketchy hearing, spots, shakiness, being closer to the sidewalk, and guarded steps. At every encounter, I feel a need to halt time because the get-togethers are so enjoyable. Joyous joke cracking mixed with mellow memories prevail. I want to savor the moments by stopping the clock.

Friendship has never been governed by the passage of time. (Here we go with that Time thing again). Should we stop noticing details when we know time is running out? Or dare we notice them even more because of it? Do details matter as we grow older? Do we care about a droopy lip, hesitant speech, more lines accenting that droopy lip, and a twist of the head to pick up the word?

We meet plenty of people in a lifetime. Family, for better or for worse, is forever. We meet numerous strangers. Some become friends; among them a few best friends. Being someone's friend is nice, but having a best friend is, well, the best.

Friendship should not be measured by how often people spend time together, or by how much they have in common. It's not defined by simply labeling someone your friend (or by being on Facebook). Friendship is about kindness, compassion, and caring about another, regardless of how much time you spend together.

When someone is your friend, and you theirs, you know it; never question it, and treasure it.

The Days Get Longer by a Minute

My father adjusted to the winter and the December solstice with his oft-repeated phrase, "Shortest day of the year. From now on, every day will become longer by one minute." Peter and I glanced at each other and snickered when he said it. Now we say it every year, particularly on those long winter days that seem to endure for more than ever.

I believe we do it not only to remember him, but more so to reflect on his optimism, his eager sprint, albeit slowly, to the first day of baseball's spring training and his beloved Red Sox. He and I watched many of my kids' baseball games during what was supposed to be April weather, good enough to play ball. So many times, while we watched, we retreated to the car, turned on the engine and the heater to warm. Our winter coats, scarves, and gloves were not enough to ward off the cold from painful toes and frosted fingertips. A 'crack of the bat' was a crack indeed, batters shaking their gloved hands as they sprinted to first base.

As we sat in the car, you might predict what Dad said? You bet. Spreading his gloved hands, "Every day gets longer by a minute," laughing with the joke of the kids playing a baseball game in forty-degree weather. Frost notwithstanding, the game continued as did he.

As I reflect on it, I realize there is a message to what he said. At the solstice, the sun is at its lowest angle in the sky, sending its shortest amount of daylight and warming energy. Nights are the longest. But the earth is tilting the other way, the sun will get higher and longer days are approaching. Sure, it's a slow process, but crocuses will soon stir in their winter beds.

The ancients celebrated the solstice as a turning point – the day that marks the return of the sun. So too did my Dad. For him, the solstice was more than a long, cold, dreary day with no end. It meant he was getting closer to spring, albeit slowly. It was an important milestone; the shortest day and the longest night signaling a transition, a change of season to be commemorated, as did the ancients. For them, the winter solstice celebrated the longest hours of darkness but more so, the continuing rebirth of the sun and its energy that meant regeneration, renewal, and reflection.

Make your transition from the shortest day to a longer moment of quiet energy wherein you focus on your intentions for the coming year. Examine and let go of your past distractions and poor decisions. Make changes. As the bats awaken, you too should feel their sting.

Celebrate. Resolve. Renew. As the light of the day gets longer, get outside, take a walk even if it's cold. Embrace it. Don't complain.

And then get yourself to a warm space. Anticipate the crack of the bat. Spring is closer by a minute each day.

CHAPTER VII

FOOD

Of Tortillas and Omelets to Die For

There were many reasons for us to anticipate our trip to Spain … geography, culture, history, art, music, etc. And food, of course. Though *jamón*, ham, was at the top of our list, I did not realize how often tortillas, the egg-based omelet *(tortilla patate)* was served. We encountered it at every breakfast and in every bar and restaurant.

We took a cooking class in Barcelona with Chef Alvaro Brun, and the first dish we prepared was the tortilla.

It reminded me of the days when my mother made potatoes and egg sandwich for my lunch. The Spanish omelet is thick, but it did not match my mother's.

High school lunches were an anticipated part of the school day, sometimes an adventure. Our group had enviable and interesting sandwiches … contents nestled in rich textured bread, wholesome aromas permeating the lunchroom. Any sandwich, pepper, and eggs, Italian cold cuts, baloney and mustard, peanut butter, and jelly, eggplant and meatballs might come out of those lunch bags that our mothers prepared, but when they went Italian, it was a different story.

Of all that Mom made, the one I loved best was the potato and egg frittata. I knew what I had on my way to school because the lunch bag was as heavy as a book. She put the monster in a number eight or nine bag, among the biggest Kraft made.

At the lunch table, I took the sandwich out and removed the wax paper. Mom had cut the sandwich in half, and I could see its contents. The potatoes were browned, firm and crispy and were layered in a pillow of buttery-colored egg speckled with black pepper. A thin layer of olive oil covered the creation and oozed through the bread. An occasional onion popped up. Once there were a few pieces of sausage. The full-bodied Italian bread, now weakened by the oil, softened, and split. Sometimes I punctured it with my fingers. It didn't matter. Nor did it matter that the omelet was cold. Its consistency was better. I consumed it, chewing slowly so I could savor its full taste. The potatoes were crunchy, just the way I liked them; the eggs soft, the bread a mush of flavor – pepper, oil, the smell of our kitchen.

It was Mom's forte, and it was thick!

The Spanish say, "A well-made tortilla is one of the best things you'll eat in Spain, or anywhere. They're easy-to-make and are a kind of carefully crafted comfort food that few Americans have ever had the chance to experience." Wrong. It was one I experienced early and often in my life, and I never forgot it.

Here I was, vacationing and remembering the days of my youth, thanks to the tortilla. I was not prepared to have an omelet in Spain transport me to my days in Providence, Rhode Island.

Ummm ... *delicious* ... everywhere.

Eels Are Not My Favorite

I never think of eels except at Christmas; I guess because they were served as part of La Vigilia, our traditional Christmas Eve dinner. My family loved them, some considering the dish a delicacy.

My lack of enthusiasm started when I was a kid at our summer rental on the Narragansett, R.I. shore. My uncle took me to the dock to see the fisherman catching eels one night. At eight years old, I was afraid of the dark, so perhaps the stage was set.

As they pulled the serpentine eels out of the water, I watched the slimy snakes squirm, ominously opening and closing their mouths. They were fish but had imperceptible gills, no scales, and, in the dark, no noticeable fins except for a ribbon thing along their backs.

The next time I saw them was when that same uncle's mother was making a fish sauce. Perking on her stove was a red gravy and sticking out were the antennas of squid flailing amid hunks of dark mounds. "I'm cooking squid and the darker things are *anguilla*, eels." Even in the gravy, they looked mysterious.

And then, somewhere along my educational way, I was told of the uncorroborated theory of spontaneous generation; the eel being its example. Aristotle believed that they were sexless and considered them natural originators. Our professor told us that the eels Aristotle caught were just sexually immature.

So, for this article, I did a little homework. Eels evolved fifty million years ago. To my knowledge, no one has ever seen eels spawning, so it is difficult to understand how they reproduce.

Every American and European eel is born in the middle of the Atlantic Ocean, the Sargasso Sea south of Bermuda. The warm, salty, calmer conditions in the Sargasso make it ideally suited for spawning. Every year, after hatching, the tiny eels swim off toward land and up the coast to the rivers, spending their juvenile and adult lives in freshwater. At the end of their lives, they return to the sea to reproduce and die.

When they return to the Sargasso, they carry only enough fat and protein for a one-way trip. The trip is not easy thanks to thousands of dams along the eastern seaboard. Juveniles make it upstream with the aid of fish ladders but face the danger of being chewed up by the turbines in hydropower dams on their way back down as adults.

The population is dwindling due to coastal development, overfishing, dams, disease, predation, and consumption. Thousands of tons of eel are consumed annually.

It would be nice if eels could be raised in substantial numbers, but to date, this has not happened. If the American eel population gets down to a million, it will be in grave danger.

I started by writing that I did not like to eat eels. I do appreciate, however, there are others who do. And it does not mean I do not like them as a species. I want them to last another fifty million years.

So, enjoy your eels this Christmas, but please, in moderation.

Eat Your Lentils

Most every culture celebrates the New Year, and Italy is no different. Among the many traditional customs are those that promise to bring wealth and banish bad luck.

Some years ago, we journeyed to Umbria and the Italian hill town of Castellucio (near Norcia) in the Apennine Mountains. The tranquil village lies above the plain. As we traveled above tree line, we looked up at people hang gliding and down on fertile valleys lavishly colored with red poppies, yellow rapeseed and acres of bushy, pale blue flowered lentils. Yes, lentils. The town is known for its excellent production.

I think of that beautiful village of one hundred and fifty inhabitants at New Year because of the Italian custom that reveres lentils. New Year's Day is celebrated with those lens-shaped, high protein, high fiber legumes that denote hoped for prosperity. They symbolize little coins; the more lentils, the more coins one might realize in the year to come.

There is another Italian tradition celebrated at the New Year. You may remember the film Cinema Paradiso and the scene wherein Salvatore (Toto) professes his love in his desperate pursuit of Elena.

"I'm in love with you."

"You're sweet, and I like you very much. But I don't love you."

"I don't care. I'll wait for you to fall in love with me." Then Salvatore reveals his plan: "Every night after work I'll wait for you under your window."

Salvatore begins his nightly wait in April and is still there on a snowy New Year's Eve of 1954; nine months! On New Year's Eve, at the countdown to the stroke of midnight, while he is waiting outside Elena's home, the Italians open their windows and with fireworks in the background, they throw out their old dishes, pots, and pans. It is a custom that symbolizes the need to throw out the old and to prepare for the new. My grandmother, averse to creating a neighborhood scene, just wrapped a dish in a mopine (dish cloth), placed it on the table and smashed it with a hammer.

Love, lentils, fireworks, pots, pans, and dishes; a masterful scene by director Giuseppe Tornatore.

At the New Year's Eve dinner, some Italians eat cotechino con lenticchie (sausages and green lentils) at the stroke of midnight. The sausages, high in fat content, are sliced to resemble coins and marry with the lentils ... *un abbondanza,* to symbolize riches. Our dinner, eaten early in the evening, was finished off with fruit, grapes, and roasted chestnuts, always chestnuts.

The New Year will come and, with eagerness and expectation, engender optimism for prosperity and good health.

I love this final stanza from Helen Hunt Jackson's poem, "New Year's Morning."

> *Only a night from old to new;*
> *Only a sleep from night to morn.*
> *The new is but the old come true;*
> *Each sunrise sees a new year born.*

I wish a Happy, Healthy and Bountiful New Year to you and your family!

Eat your lentils.

Time for Hot Chocolate

Last week, because it was thirty degrees with a howling wind, it became hot chocolate weather. It was not with any deductive reasoning like, "Gee, it's the first frigid day, and I need a hot chocolate," that I felt the need. No, it just happened.

I was meeting someone at the Seven Stars Bakery with coffee in mind when the young woman asked what I wanted. I blurted, "A hot chocolate, please." With that, it became winter.

A young man made one of the best hot chocolates I have had. As a first step toward banishing the winter chill, I sat and wrapped my hands around the mug letting the pure warmth flow through my fingers and palms. I gazed at the frothy foam floating at the top and then sinking to iceberg depth as it melted into the chocolate. It was time for the first sip. Anything frothy must be good.

The dark chocolate, tinged with sweet, milky foam singed my lips. Its rich flavor coated my tongue as I swirled and swallowed. I was warmed from within. A bit of foam mustached my upper lip. I looked around the bakery and then let it sit a while before licking it off. The cocoa was as good as my mother's and reminded me of the days when she made it for me after a frigid day of sledding.

Mom called it cocoa. With a tablespoon, she scooped the powder from the box of Hershey's and turned it into the milk heating on the stove. She stirred patiently and when done, she poured the cocoa into my cup and topped it with a marshmallow. I was careful to be sure the heat passed my sensitive tongue quickly as I had temporarily stuck it (and removed it painfully) on the rim of my cold sled while waiting to slide at the top of the hill. Once by my tongue, the drink's warmth trickled to my toes.

I have made hot chocolate at home by adding hot water to a prescribed mix. Though good, it hardly matched that of Mom's or Seven Stars'. So, I got in touch with Brian, the Seven's beverage manager who was so kind to share their recipe. They use cocoa powder, cane sugar and a pinch of salt, adding the mix and milk to a small saucepan. They whisk it over low heat.

Once warmed, surely with love, they gradually add more milk and whisk again until hot, taking care not to boil. Vanilla extract and whipped cream seals the deal. Brian added that a pinch of cinnamon or peppermint extract instead of vanilla is also quite good.

Most of the time, we don't fuss like that with our hot chocolate because we're too busy. It's okay but every now and then, someone must fuss for us. It is a winter special. Some things are too good to have just once.

Plants Taste Like Beef. So What?

So, what's the big deal with a plant that tastes like a hamburger? Will you be eating plant-based beef soon? You might be interested in an article, *Value Meal*, by Tad Friend in the September 30 issue of *The New Yorker*. There, he discusses a potential move to eating more plant-based food, beef replicas. That's right, a beef-tasting burger that's does not beef but looks and tastes like it because of the use of heme (a genetically modified yeast that imparts the color and the taste to the creation), wheat, coconut oil, and potatoes. Little of this is new. The Impossible Whopper is already available at Burger King.

Dr. John Harvey Kellogg of Corn Flakes fame invented and sold Protose, a tasteless, flat mixture of nuts and gluten which he claimed resembled chicken, or veal. Bland food was important to Kellogg, but it was the bowel that got his undivided medical attention. Dr. Kellogg was an eccentric physician, considered a quack by many because of his whacky beliefs that the colon might be the basis of all ills, including psychiatric. Believing the colon to be a sewer of autointoxication, he recommended colonic cleansing (see the movie *Road to Wellville*). In some cases, he even recommended a total colectomy. Snap, cracked, and popped he was.

This is all so interesting because of our naïve belief that we live in an age of disruption where so much has changed like no other era. I say naïve because change has been prevalent in every era, at the turn of every century, not just ours.

Would someone transported through time from one hundred years ago believe what they were seeing; television, the internet, space travel, jet planes. Would someone from two hundred years ago believe that there might be railroads, guns that fired more than one shot at a time, enough to kill scores of people in a moment? That there would be steamships, wireless communication, *vis a vis* Marconi's inventions, the telephone in the following century? Was it not only 500 or so years ago that Copernicus and Galileo put forward the theory that the earth revolved around the sun?

There is more to the disruptive idea. I think of the Fermi Paradox, named after physicist Enrico Fermi. Simplistically, he believed that with so many planets in the Milky Way and so many like earth, there must be life out there as in "Where is everybody?" There are billions of stars in the galaxy, maybe two million galaxies just like earth. There must be, or there is about to be, interplanetary travel not originating on our earth.

Railroads, steamships, jet planes, life on other planets … innovation, invention, forward-thinking; nothing new. We have lived with disruptive forever.

So, what's the big deal about plants that taste like beef? When the plant burger made with heme is slapped on the grill, it turns from red to brown. It also looks, sizzles, and tastes like meat.

So, what's the issue?

What's Not to Like About Roasted Chestnuts

I was on Fifth Avenue in New York and from around a corner, I recognized that smell ... toasty, charbroiled, earthy, and nutty. I made the turn and spotted the vendor in front of his hot, saucer-shaped pan loaded with roasting chestnuts. Whorls of steamy scents rose between the buildings. People huddled closer and rubbed their hands together. Our seller stopped turning his ladle only to fill a cone-shaped newspaper with the treats. When he handed them over, I thought I heard whimpers. I thought of Italy.

My cousin Vincenzo, who lives just north of Naples in Roccamonfina, with his wife Anna, is the proprietor of a chestnut farm. Diane and I had the good fortune to visit them some years ago.

People were harvesting chestnuts on every open plot of land. The edible chestnut is the one familiar at holidays; easy to spot in its spiny, needle-sharp husk. The inedible, back yard horse chestnut that we knew as kids, has a smoother husk and was good only for the game of kingers.

Vincenzo: *"Tuo nonno ha vissuto vicino a una fattoria di castagne."* (Your grandfather lived nearby on a chestnut farm.). I loved his lilting Italian. "However, when he emigrated to America, he lost his rights." I stared into space. "You mean I could have inherited a chestnut farm! In Italy! I could have been a chestnut farmer in Italy!" Oh well ...

Chestnuts also come to mind when I think of La Vigilia. They are the end of meal staple of that marvelous Christmas Eve feast. At the end of the abbondanza came the chestnuts that had been roasted on the Barstow Stove top. Grandpa cut them so that they would roast evenly and open without a burst. Using his sharpened jackknife, he scored them with an "X" on the rounded side and placed them on the stove with the flatter side down. Grandma lightly laced them with olive oil.

Roasted chestnuts were the food that complemented the meal. Grandma brought them to the table mounded in a large dish.

They opened enough so that when they cooled, they were easy to peel. There are two reasons to eat a chestnut right away. The longer you wait to remove the shell, the harder the work will be. So, what if your fingers burn and you must cool the treat with a blow? When opened, the firm, spongy, soft nut was easily breakable.

The second reason? They were delicious when warm.

Notwithstanding the fact that we had eaten for hours and thought we were satisfied, we started on the chestnuts. We shook the hot ones in our cupped hands. Then we ate more. Mounds of chestnut skins were centered on the table.

I recognized how good the chestnut was, but not until recent years did, I realize how healthy (low fat, high protein, gluten-free, high in vitamins and fiber) they are.

Chestnuts remind me of a day in New York, our visit with Vincenzo and Anna, and La Vigilia.

Learning to Cook, Starting a Business, and Giving Back

Diane and I love to go to the Farmer's Market at the Mt. Hope Farm in Bristol, especially in the winter when they host it in the barn. It's a cozy outbuilding, walled with old siding and ceilinged by a hanging loft. The vendors and the patrons are welcomed by soothing, soft music being played at the far end, just in front of the warming fireplace.

Upon entering, we are comforted by the aromas of burning wood, fresh bread, honey, coffee, and apple cider. After our initial purchases of bread and honey, we moseyed to the "Secrets in the Kitchen" table where Karen Greene was selling her delicious marinara sauce.
We jumped at it. And we chatted. I was intrigued by her story, one of enthusiasm, perseverance, and skill. Karen's passion for her sauce, made with fresh ingredients from her garden, is well founded. We have returned for more.

For years, Karen spent every Sunday in the kitchen watching her mom cook the family dinner. Karen learned from her while hearing the story of Karen's grandfather, a carpenter and cook who grew his ingredients and raised the animals for the lamb sausages on his large plot of land. He was born in Lebanon and immigrated to America where he met his French-Canadian wife.

In later years Karen, fortified by the "aroma" of her history, created, and perfected her "Secrets in the Kitchen Marinara Sauce," her first commercial kitchen product. Her efforts were aided and encouraged by the principals at Hope and Main, Warren, Rhode Island's food incubator business. The sauce has been a favorite of many who have passed through the Hope and Main kitchens and/or visited farmers' markets.

Hope and Main and its founders, Lisa Raiola, and Waterman Brown, have continued to guide Karen. Now, not only does Karen Greene teach pasta-making classes there, but she has also joined the Nourish our Neighbors "Buy One, Give One," a splendid civic service offered by the marvelous community-oriented folks based there. Karen will cook family sized dinners, and for each person who buys one meal, another is sent to someone in need in the community. We have ordered from them and have never been disappointed.

In recent weeks, their arms of philanthropy have reached far and wide. The program provides free ready-to-eat meals made by member companies using wholesome and local ingredients. I spoke with Lisa and Waterman this week, and to date, Hope & Main has distributed 13,584 meals since the outset of this program. Stunning!

There are so many things one might say about The Hope and Main incubator for those wishing to get into the food business. Ingenuity with enthusiasm is their trademark, but it goes even further. Just look at Karen Greene's path ... learning to cook at home, honing her skills, creating a business at Hope and Main, selling pasta sauce, teaching, and now giving back to the community. What a fine example to set for many.

What Is Your Favorite Pie?

One of my favorite things to do when I was a kid was to go to downtown Providence with my mother on a Saturday. And one of the many highlights of the day was our stop at the Boston Store where we sat at the soda fountain, and I had custard pie and milk. It was worth being dragged around from store to store to finally reach that oasis.

To this day, I remember the delectable pie with its firm crust and soft, silky, creamy-cold taste. To wash it down with the ice-cold milk was a bonus.

My memory and appreciation of that pie came to mind when I read an article in the *Smithsonian Magazine* about the origin and love of pie in America. Initially, it was not an easy love affair because pie-eating was reserved for immigrants and lower classes. Soon, however, the craze took off and pie became America's favorite dessert, moving far beyond the kidney and mincemeat pies the New England settlers ate. The 'new' pie was sweetened, filled with fruits, and cuddled by lighter and flakier crusts.

During WWI, pie took on a symbolic significance and was now considered patriotic. Craving for pie became a "hunger for democracy" wrote a reporter in a Boston Globe editorial of 1918. By the turn of the century, Americans were eating more apple pie than any other variety … "as American as apple pie" went the phrase, as nostalgic as baseball and hot dogs. Here is today's statistic: 186 million pies are purchased each year in the United States.

My love of pie grew beyond the custard of the downtown trip. It was reinvigorated when Mom made the Blueberry Table Talk Pie an integral part of every lunch. What a delightful surprise to open my lunch bag to find that prize. I placed it on the table as I ate my baloney and mustard sandwich, knowing my treat was nearby, like a security blanket.

How nicely that little baby fit into my hand. How savory to bite into the center, spilling sweetness along my cheeks. How soft and flaky was the buttery crust.

Table Talk Pies of Worcester, MA, was started in 1924 by two Greek immigrants. Through a combination of demanding work and perseverance, the founders of the company, Mr. Theodore Tonna and Mr. Angelo Cotsidas, managed to build the solid foundation of a business that is today one of our country's leading pie companies. How very ironic it is that pie, once considered something only for the downtrodden, made those immigrants so successful and vaulted the pie to such status.

In my junior high school days, we frequented The Table Talk Pie Bakery in Providence to fill our coffers for the week.

Well, do you know what America's' favorite pies are today? I was a bit surprised to learn that cherry, chocolate cream, pumpkin and you bet ... apple, were the top four. Where was my beloved blueberry? Or custard?

What's your favorite?

Shifting Blame in the Middle of Chaos

As I listen to so many people unabashedly assigning blame during this coronavirus outbreak, I think of something that happened to me when I was a kid. One day, while playing street soccer, one of the other kids kicked a ball that went off my shoulder and headed toward the window of one of our jumpier neighbors. The ball crashed through the window and, as soon as I saw it, I knew we would one day be taking a trip to Benny's with window on wagon to get it repaired. A fast-stepping, buxom woman in a black dress and with a needle through her hair bun emerged, rolling pin in hand, screaming, "Who did this? Who did this? I'm calling the police."

The kicker pointed to me and cried, "He did. Right there. That kid.

He did it." Though initially, I was willing to accept part of the responsibility, I was stunned as he shunted all of it to me!

"Why did you blame me when we are both responsible?" Shoulders slumped, he looked at his Keds. Even at ten years old, I knew he no longer could be a close friend. He shifted the blame.

Nowadays, there are buckets full of blame being thrown around like hot potatoes, a commodity that few wish to catch. It seems more a strategy: throw the blame on someone else's wall to see if it will stick. It is unsettling.

Simply put, blame is to consider someone else responsible for a misdeed, a failure, or an undesirable outcome. "Our team did what we had to. It was the coach's fault for the loss." "Don't blame me. You made the decision." "Who? Me?" Common refrains.

Is dispatching blame to another appropriate? Is it acceptable? Warranted? Like many things in life, our drill of blaming is often done for the wrong reason, at the wrong time, in an inappropriate manner or, even worse, for the wrong ethics. What happened to integrity? Or conscience?

We are in the middle of a crisis that is taking the lives of our citizens. There are many reasons why, when, and where it happened. Is that important now, particularly since our country is in a misdirected chaos? Should that be the focus garnering so much attention, particularly since we need to direct our energies to a plan to make people better, to saving lives! To making a plan?!

We should be inspired by leaders who convey confidence and comfort. They need to focus their attention on solutions … for us. Shunting blame bolsters negative energy. Nothing good comes from it.

Find a way to order the chaos. Correct the lack of direction. Redirect attention to positive. With all that is necessary for a country fractured by the epidemic, please, leaders, just do it.

Put your minds to solutions. To cooperation. Goodness, we have so many things that need solving.

Losing a friend because of a childhood disagreement is one thing. Losing lives is another.

Hope and Main Does It. Again

It's impossible not to get excited when you chat with Lisa Raiola and Waterman Brown, the principals of Hope and Main, in Warren, RI. They are the non-profit, premier business incubator for food and beverage companies.

The businesses are housed in a skillfully restored old elementary school, a replica of the one I attended in Providence. I had goosebumps as I smelled the oiled, wooden floors, pushed open the substantial doors, remembered the cozy classrooms and touched a brick wall like the one where I once pitched baseball cards. It was pure nostalgia that set the tone for the delight inside.

Hope and Main is helping to grow the local economy by creating support for food entrepreneurs while cultivating an environment where startups can test, create, and thrive. The enthusiasm of the excited entrepreneurs was readily apparent. Hope and Main has reached even further.

With the onset of the COVID epidemic, Lisa, Waterman, and the staff rose to the occasion of need, with nothing more than a goal of helping their community. They started with the donor and grant (RI Foundation) supported, Nourish Our Neighbors program.

For the past twelve weeks, five days a week from 8:00 am to 11:00 am, they have served as a distribution point for grab and go meals prepared by the Bristol Warren School District for eligible food-insecure families. Three days a week, they supplement the grab and go meals with meals prepared by a rotating squad of marvelous member companies at the Hope & Main facility. These young chefs prepare over six thousand meals each week, serving 200 to 300 meals each day: near 7,000 in total.

Once each week, they deliver prepared meals to the Senior Centers in Bristol, Warren, and Barrington and to vulnerable, food-insecure seniors throughout the East Bay; near 2,000 in total.

They have provided prepared meals to the Women's Resource

Center (transitional housing for women and children victims of domestic violence), and to L.I.F.E. Inc. for developmentally disabled adults living in residential settings and group homes.

One month ago, Hope and Main began to offer a community meal-share program called "Buy One/Give One." Meals can be purchased for $16, with half the proceeds going back to the Nourish Our Neighbors program. For that cost, one meal will be available for the purchaser to pick up on Mondays, from 4-7 pm, and one meal will be reserved for a community member. This sustains the program while promoting an equitable food system. The food entrepreneur offering the meal varies each week. We have partaken, and every meal has been wonderful.

To date, Hope & Main has distributed almost 16,000 meals.

Says Raiola, "One of the silver linings of the crisis has been the opportunity for so many new, young chefs to shine. There are several entrepreneurs who have even launched their businesses during this pandemic. They are enthusiastic, mission-driven, problem solvers who love the opportunity to serve the community."

Thank you, Hope and Main. You have made, and are making, a difference.

The Mt. Hope Farm Contributes

I am encouraged by the many contributions that people and organizations are making to their communities in these challenging times. If you just scratch the surface, you will find people doing good things for their fellow man around every corner. The Mt. Hope Farm in Bristol is one of those.

I enjoy going to The Farm. I am lucky to be a member of its Board. With its bucolic setting, roaming animals, serpentine trails, sturdy barns, location by the bay and gardens, it is exciting, inviting and quite peaceful. This day, urged by Jon Feinstein's, "You know, they grow a ton of vegetables every year and send it to The Food Bank," I visited the vegetable gardens and its curators while thinking, "My goodness! A ton?"

I strolled past the sheds and the greenhouse to the welcoming gate of the gardens. With a gentle push, I walked to an area that Poet Laureate Robert Frost would have loved. Ordered and peaceful, busy chirping birds and a few bleats from contented goats, welcomed me. Beehives were nestled in the far trees and just beyond was the hum of traffic. Every day on this beautiful farm, urban meets rural in most surprising ways.

I had been in this garden before, but under different circumstances. It was the setting for a remarkable fundraising cocktail party. Socializing distracted me then, but not now. The gardens were hushed; two women were working in silence.

Nancy Stratton and Beth Battey looked up from their work of planting. They have been volunteering in the gardens since directing the building of the beds some years ago. To my right was a table of inviting, freshly picked large radishes. I walked among the perfectly ordered raised beds; near each were seedlings, winter-nurtured in the greenhouse by Nancy and Beth, ready for their allotted spots. Yes, I had heard correctly. One ton of food per summer, fresh produce every Friday to The East Bay Food Pantry in Bristol. "Vegetables to market." What a nice ring that had.

Much like The Victory Gardens (food gardens for defense) of WWI and II where governments encouraged people to plant to supplement rations, aid the war efforts and boost morale, The Mt. Hope Farm was on the same path of reducing pressure on the public food supply while reaping the satisfying rewards of produce.

The Mt. Hope Farm vegetable garden works in conjunction with The URI Master Gardner's program; Larry Ashley is the coordinator. URI donates plants and sends volunteers who help to fulfill their mission to educate citizens in environmentally-sound gardening practices through the dissemination of factual, research-based information.

Nancy and Beth volunteer at The Farm every Wednesday and Friday; hands in the dirt, smiling with a need-based purpose. I asked what they, in turn, might need. "Volunteers, we need volunteers. And we would be remiss if we did not say financial support."

One ton a year. Thank you, Mt. Hope Farm. You are making a difference.

CHAPTER VIII

HUMOR

A Surprise in the Bowling Alley

I was introduced to bowling when growing up in the Mt. Pleasant neighborhood of Providence. A friend, who was a pinsetter ("pin boy") at an alley in the Olneyville section, within walking distance of my home, introduced me to the game. He was paid ten cents a string to set the pins after they were knocked down.

The targets were duckpins, fired at with a small, softball-sized, light ball with no finger holes. The ball fit comfortably in the palm of my hand. With three rolls per frame, we learned the words "strike" and "spare" and how to score. We rented shoes.

My later memories were of going bowling on a date. It was an easy date … not much you had to say, anxiety quashed by activity, ice cream and then home. Yes, yes … home.

In these, my more mature years, I bowl on occasion with my grandchildren, using a bigger, heavier ball with three holes in it for fingers and thumb. The object is the same – to knock down as many pins as possible.

I have realized a few things. First, the gutters on either side of the alley gobble balls quicker than they ever did when I was younger. Second, the alleys are heavily oiled. Third, I ache after bowling.

On this day, I wanted to show the kids that I could curve the ball and hit the pocket between the one and three pin, the way I saw the world champ do it on TV when I was a kid. "Pay attention, kids! Watch me curve this one into the pocket for a strike!"

I bent over to swipe the alley with my fingers. "Hmmm," I thought. "I don't remember this much oil." I dried my hands on the nearby blower as the ball made its way to me along the aqueduct.

I picked it up, squeezed my fingers in, walked back as far as I could, took my run, swung my arm back and tried to let the missile go. I stuttered to a dead stop at the foul line and, as the stubborn ball snapped out, I lurched and, yep, you guessed it. With a minimal degree of difficulty, I flew, spread-eagled, into the alley, sliding effortlessly along the well-oiled surface on my belly. I lay there saturated in my share of oil.

The bowling crew, patrons, Diane, and grandkids came running, bleating words I did not want to hear. "Are you alright, sir?" It's the "sir" thing that got me; a word that defined me as a senior citizen subject to the dreaded fall.

"Yes, Yes, I'm fine, I'm fine," as I snapped to my knees. I looked down the alley to see that honey of a ball hit the one-three pocket for a strike!

I stood, turned with the swagger of a gunslinger, wiped my hands on my pants and shirt, blew on my fingers, looked to my grandchildren, now bent with laughter, and declared, "Now, that's how you do it, kids."

The Old Guy Is In Good Shape

For years, I told my patients to control what they were able to control. I listed the usual ... no smoking, no alcohol to excess, maintain a fit weight, exercise regularly, drive judiciously, mitigate stress, and treat your body like a shrine ... no foreign substances and no piercing.

Though it wasn't always easy, I tried to set an example; exercise being one of my imperatives. When the "belong to a gym" popularity started, I joined. There was little else in those early fitness centers save for machines; the kind that test strength, tempt you to push harder, add weights, get a hernia, and feel good because it hurts.

I went often enough to hurt. I added more weights each time so that I could feel the pain. "Oooo, that feels ... err ... good." Wasn't that the point? To hurt? To never want to go back. To feel whole once you were finished with the punishment.

I flexed my muscles, looked in the mirrors on every wall and was proud of myself until one auspicious day. I went to the gym early to get it over with and go on to work. After a warmup, I started my trek from apparatus to apparatus, reviewing the account card in hand and adjusting the weights accordingly.

I was sailing along (at least I thought so) and by the fourth machine, an overhead push, I felt good, limber, crescents of sweat staining my shirt under my neck and underarms, biceps bulging (sorta) and ready to strip the gears. There were enough mirrors to satisfy my ego. After all, is that not the point? To see what you think are your bulging muscles. Abuse the machine, stand, look in the mirror, flex one biceps, then the other, then both, all the while looking at yourself. Were those mirrors magnifiers?

I sat, pushed my back against the pad, bent my arms, grabbed the bars with my sweaty palms and pushed again, and again. Oh, and with a grunt of course, "Uooargghh, uh." I was a monster. Just as I was in the middle of my reps, two young men walked through on their way to the locker room. They glanced at me.

Sensing an audience, my grunts now intensified with an additional "Oo-ahh-arghh" added to the first "Uooargghh." It was a good thing I was strapped in.

One young man said to his friend, "That old guy on the machines ain't bad."

"Nope. In decent shape for an old guy."

I looked around for the old guy and saw no one. It was early. Wait! There was an old guy! It was me! I saw me in the mirror.

My grunts faded to oblivion. My muscles contracted to mushy spindles, now hurting more than ever. I stopped, exhaled, and paused.

Oh well. This old guy sure felt good. Couldn't wait to get home to the marvelous menthol, camphor bouquet of Ben Gay.

A Surprise in the Doctor's Office

I didn't want to call the doctor for a pain in my toe, but it woke me in the middle of the night. Knowing too much but not enough, I was sure I had something serious, perhaps lethal. I became haunted by the thought of a galloping infection that would become systemic, untreatable, and all-consuming.

I called the next morning for the appointment. As I approached the doctor's building, I grew confident, because of the visit, unexpectedly helped by the edifice … a rectangular, solid block of bricks and cement with windows set back in the four stories like a bunker; a concrete stronghold that would last forever.

I rode to the third floor on an efficient elevator, limped to the office, checked in, sat, changed my seat away from a coughing patient not covering her mouth and was called before I had a chance to open my phone for messages, waiting no more than five minutes.

I was escorted to the examining room, sat, looked around at the diplomas, took off my shoe and sock, took out my phone again and sat barely two minutes when the very professional-looking (neat, pressed white coat, crisp shirt, matching up-to-date tie, polished shoes) doctor came in. We chatted, small talk ... family, vacations, weather, and sports. His expertise and engagement relaxed me. I was confident that he would take good care.

He sat and just as he slid his stool over to look at my toe, the fire alarm went off. "Let's go. Out." Sock on, unlaced shoe on. As I walked out of the office, I went by the kitchen, and there I saw a smoking microwave spilling out a toasty odor of something left forgotten, vaporized. Smoke filled the room, triggering the efficient detector, b ... eee ... p, b ... eee ... p ... as it should. I walked down the stairs following a herd of relaxed, carefree patients and employees.

Outside, in the cold, I tied my shoe. Three trucks arrived in minutes, blaring sirens. Firemen dressed in long fireproof coats, thick heavy pants, and long bright yellow jackets, gloves, boots, durable helmets with shields on the front and bearing apparatuses like tanks, axes, and crowbars, poured in like a swat team. They oozed confidence. With no surprise, they found the source and out they came within minutes.

"All clear."

Back I went to the office, repeated the sock off process and in came the doctor who looked at my toe and asked, "Do you walk in cold weather?"

"Yes"

"Chilblains."

"Chilblains?"

"Yes, chilblains. Probably related to the cold. It's like a small burn at the end of your toe. Just dress it with a salve. You'll be fine."

"Great. Neat diagnosis. Thank you!" Whew. I would live.

Out he went. "Let me know if you have any problems." I was confident, content, pleased.

As I was donning my sock, he propped open the door. "I forgot the pizza in the microwave. I tripped the alarm."

Laughter unseated my painful toe.

The Day Started Well

The day started well but drifted a bit toward afternoon. Diane and I were excited to be going to the Isabella Stewart Gardner Museum in Boston. It is one of our favorites, and this day we were going to see the Botticelli exhibit.

We were not disappointed. The museum castle surrounds landscaped gardens with a peripheral hopscotch of rooms chock full of treasures ... extensive collections of European, Asian, and American paintings, sculptures, tapestries, furniture, manuscripts, rare books, architectural fragments, and decorative arts.

The Botticellis were a surprise. Crisp, captivating, and detailed, the stories created in his paintings were considered a beacon leading back to the light: Lucretia's rape led to the overthrow of the monarchy in 510 BC; Virginia's murder moved Romans to rebel against their increasingly despotic governors a few decades later. A woman's message, painful yet so relevant, delivered centuries ago.

To accompany the exhibit, the museum commissioned Karl Stevens, a well-known Boston-based graphic novelist, to add to the show; rendering Botticelli's two tales in comic-book form from the women's point of view, shifting each story from political allegory to the violent thing that it is. Two splendid educational exhibits.

We capped the morning with lunch at the Museum's café.

And then things changed. As we were driving through a less than upbeat section of Boston, our car died. Yep. Dead: dead as in we were frozen in place. I was afraid to look in the rearview mirror at the stream of stopped traffic as I heard the blaring horns. Diane called AAA. As we sat holding up what seemed like the city for forty-five minutes, we were aided by a most hospitable, neighborhood, gap-toothed, garrulous gentleman who told us that he worked for a mechanic and had a host of ideas for us to get started. I told him we'd rather wait for AAA. "OK, sure." Undaunted and industrious, he found two traffic cones, from a nearby business, placed them well to the rear of our car and directed traffic away as he called the police.

"I gotta call them or you'll get towed, and it will cost you a lot, Buddy."

"AAA is on the way," I replied.

"OK, OK." The police moseyed by, stopped a moment, looked, and coasted along as our friend stood between us. He turned to us and with a nod, smiled, "See, ya gotta take care of it."

When the tow arrived, we thanked our noble stranger for his help and rewarded him appropriately.

Now, with car on the truck's platform and us in the front seat, we trekked to the outskirts of Boston to a repair facility.

"We can't help you. Our mechanic left for the day."

Our driver, Robenson D, took careful, considerate care and delivered us to a Ford dealership in Norwood miles away. He could not have been more engaging or kind.

The dealership welcomed us, called for a rental and off we headed for home, finally.

Gardner, Botticelli, Stevens, roadside heroes ... quite a day.

Will I Ever Be Able to Whistle?

Is it too late to learn how to whistle? No, I don't mean the Lauren Bacall "Put your lips together and blow" whistle. I can do that. I can hold the pucker position for a bit and whistle a marching song. I heard the world whistle champion on NPR one day. He sounded like the symphony, whistling more notes than I could count. Forget that.

There is one other whistle in my repertoire; the one modulated with a piece of grass held between thumbs and cupped hands and blowing. A high-pitched, short-lived meaningless shrill emanates. Though the grandchildren may love it, it's not the whistle I covet.

I want the neighborhood whistle ... the loud, crisp, no-nonsense signal that opens the street and gets attention; the kind Andy's father made, a crisp ... phweep ... when he wanted him home. One whistle and Andy was running, even if he was out of sight. That's the one I want to do. I have tried and failed.

I yearn for that fingerless, attention-grabbing special, the one that is born by pursing lips and curling tongue in contorted fashion and blowing. I envy those who can just let go. I moisten my lips, conjure a sardonic grin and blow. Nothing but a wisp of silence. Harder. Deep breath in, breath out. Impossible. The wisp becomes a whoosh that only I can hear.

I've tried by sticking my fingers in the sides of my mouth. I saw some do that. A bit unsanitary but worth the risk if it worked. I tried different combinations ... right and left index, right and left middles, right and left pinkies, thumb, and index in a variety of positions. All I get is a silent saliva spill.

I've tried a variety of tongue positions ... broad tongue, flat tongue, rest it on my bottom teeth, push it on the top, close my lips, open my lips, make a 'V' shaped hole, blow through the hole. I get neither sound nor attention. I am stumped. So, I checked the internet.

There is a fair amount of information about whistling techniques. I've tried them all. It's a good thing I was not being recorded. Looking at the monitor and contorting my face in so many ways bore its share of ugliness. If I had any success, it would have been worth it, but I could never find the sweet spot. I blew until I had a headache, got dizzy or my jaws hurt.

So, I bought a good old fashioned metal whistle, the kind that looks like angel wings, the one with edges of sharp metal. When I was a kid, I had one that worked. I was able to make a bunch of different sounds, even music, sorta. These days, I can repeat a few, but when I saw blood at the sides of my mouth, I quit and threw it away.

Where can I take a whistling class?

How to Sell Your Home

Some years ago, we had a house for sale. "If you bury a statue of St. Joseph upside down in your yard, you will be guaranteed to sell your house quickly and at a favorable price."

"You're kidding." We had heard the story many times before, but we were a little concerned about using superstition, witchcraft, or fable for something so important.

"Why not try it?" Diane asked.

"Of course, what have we to lose?"

We went to a nearby variety store, one that had been part of its neighborhood for years.

"Do you have a statue of St. Joseph?" I asked.

"I think so. What do you want it for?" the benevolent elderly proprietors asked.

"Well." I was reluctant to say I wanted to bury him to sell my house.

My wife saved me. "This is First Communion time. He will make a great gift."

"Yes, yes," I said. "It's for a First Communion." It was a good thing the old store was dark enough to hide my embarrassment. As they hesitated, I was quick to say, "Never mind, never mind."

"Wait, wait, let's see. We must have one."

The old man rolled out his ancient wooden ladder which creaked and shook as he moved it from its comfortable spot. He wavered as he balanced it and then slam! The ladder hit the top shelf, rattled, and came to a stop. He climbed as a Sherpa might climb Mt. Everest.

"Let me get it," I said with urgency.

'No, no, I have it here somewhere."

He climbed to a top shelf loaded with a chorus of statues, one of St. Joseph patiently waiting under a thick layer of dust. The old man lifted it, steadied himself and blew the dust. "Please St. Joseph, protect him."

Down he came balancing the statue, one too big and too sacred to bury.

"Is this what you want? And what did you say you want it for?" He cradled it with reverence.

"I think it is a bit too big. And I'm thinking now that my Godson would like a pen and pencil set." The Cross set saved many a Godparent.

"OK," he said. Back to the sanctuary, he climbed as I bolted for the door. Diane was waiting.

"What happened?"

"Well, he had the statue, but I just could not buy it. Too big. Too sacrilegious."

"Let's try the religious goods store next to the church." I nodded.

We entered the store and again, with a sheepish look, I asked "Do you have a St. Joseph statue?"

"Sure," the lady said. "I guess you want to sell your house." I paused. "Well, if you do, we have these St. Joseph kits that tell you exactly what to do."

A kit?! I could not believe it. On the third shelf were two rows of boxed, small St. Josephs. "The instructions are inside," she said as she picked one off.

"Don't forget to bury him upside down," she called as I left the store, kit in hand.

Do You Know What Druthers Are?

Last week, a group of us met with a young lady, Eleonora, from Rome, to have her guide us in speaking better Italian. It was a marvelous session, as most anything in the Italian language seems to be. At one point, our chat revolved around the use of Italian idioms which, along with the verbs, are a difficult part of the language. Nonetheless, we need to be familiar with them to reach that next level.

Eleonora was quick to say that she was having the same problems with English idioms ... "a dime a dozen, bite the bullet and better late than never," to name a few. No surprise. For some reason, I thought of the word druthers; one I learned years ago when reading Al Capp's *L'il Abner*. "I'm sure you have not heard anything like the word druthers."

"Druthers?" she asked with her enviable Roman inflection. "Whatt, do you mean?" I love the way she finished the word "whatt;" distinctively European.

I told her of a scene in the musical, *L'il Abner* when a group of Dogpatch people sat around to sing "If I Had My Druthers." Though he may have popularized it, cartoonist Al Capp did not coin the term. The earliest reference is from 1833. Etymologist Barry Popick tracked down this quote in an issue of *American Turf Register and Sporting Magazine*: "I'd druther live in the woods anytime by myself than on the best plantation in the country."

In Mark Twain's 1896 novel *Tom Sawyer, Detective,* Huck Finn says to Tom, "Any way you'd druther have it, that is the way I'd druther have it." When Tom responds, he uses druther as a noun. "There ain't any druthers about it Huck Finn. Nobody said anything about druthers."

Druther is a modification of "would rather," as in I would rather or I'd rather. The example of shifting a sound from one component phrase to another is called metanalysis. Druthers is just a term that simply reflects an informality of tone, not a lack of sophistication or education. If you saw the musical or read the comic strip, you might think otherwise.

So, I told Eleonora about *L'il Abner* and proceeded with a less formal explanation. "I would rather" contracts to I'd druther.

"I still do nott understand." Again, that envious lilt and the pronunciation of the end of the word "nott."

"OK. If you say 'would rather' quickly enough, you might understand how these two words blur together as d'rather and then to druther. When someone says 'if I had my druthers,' they're talking about what they would do if they had a choice. When you are asked what you would like to do, you might say 'I'd rather do.' That's a druther."

"Meraviglioso. Grazie."

If we students of Italian had our druthers, we would spend more time in learning the language and the lilt, flexing our dialectal muscles with pride, and pronouncing the endd of every wordd.

Articulation with an Italian lilt. Nothing I'd druther do.

My Brief Time on a Pony

In my previous article about the Narragansett Racetrack, I wrote that I had little experience with horses prior to seeing them race. Well, that is not true. I did have an experience with a nasty pony at Roger Williams Park in Providence when I was ten years old.

On most Sundays, I was led around the dusty oval track by a tight-lipped lady. Oh, the boredom of riding on a gloomy pony led by a depressed woman in scruffy cowboy boots, wearing a plaid wool shirt, a sweat-stained cowboy hat, a bulky flannel jacket, and threadbare dungarees held by a big-buckled belt. On this afternoon, I thought, "This is the day I ride the pony on my own."

I was dressed in my Sunday clothes, the ones Mom prescribed … pleated pants, a matching jacket, Buster Brown shoes, and a white shirt. As I handed the lady my ticket, I beamed, "I'm riding alone."

Detached, she droned, "Yep. Alone. Sure. OK. That one." She pointed to a docile, jet-black pony frothing while biting on his bit.

"What's his name?"

"Uh, yuh, 'Lightnin'."

"Lightnin'!" As I patted his neck, he pulled back, jolted, and drove his front feet deep into the dirt. Foam speckled the air. The horse lady took the reins from the post and barked, "Git 'er on up on 'im."

"On? Up?"

"Yep. C'mon, kid. Put yer foot in." I slid my Buster Brown in the stirrup. With her large hand on my butt, she gave me a boost. I whisked my right foot over the saddle and positioned the matching

Buster Brown in the other stirrup. Lightnin's ears snapped back. His nostrils flared. "Er ya on 'im?" she droned. I choked the saddle horn.

"Whaja say?"

"Er … ya … on … 'im? Dern it. Dunt yer unnerstan Inglish? Grab the rins." Before I could settle, she hit his rump and Lightnin' took off with hooves propelling sand on high. I never had the chance to grab the reins. The charger became a beast, raw power, a Derby winner, sand flying everywhere.

I was bopping in the saddle like sliding down the stairs on my butt when he slammed into the rail. As my shoe came out of the stirrup, my foot swung around to the matching Buster Brown still caught in the other stirrup. Sitting sidesaddle, I waved at the horn only to grab his mane.

A final mustang kick and I was in the air, thrown to the other side of the fence like a bolt of electricity. Thump. From my seat, I watched the pony stop at the next bend, now as calm as a grazing cow. I jumped up dazed and bewildered. I brushed myself off, climbed the fence and ran across the track where Dad was waiting. "Too much horse, Edward?"

"No, he wasn't! She never gave me a chance to get set in the saddle. It was her fault." I put my hands in my pockets and walked head down to the car.

Why Wear a Necktie?

I once met a friend who asked, "Why are you wearing a necktie? Nobody wears them anymore." I explained to him that I learned from my Dad. He never left the house, be it to go to the bank or the shoemaker or to visit his friends, without being well-dressed, the necktie a sartorial part of his garb. I was not as compulsive as he, though I felt underdressed if I went without.

Dad tied two knots … the Windsor, invented by the Duke, which

I rarely used, or the simple flip over and under, my choice.

How, when, and why did the necktie come to be such an important part of a man's wardrobe? Likely, it originated in the 17th century during the 30-year war in France. King Louis XIII hired Croatian mercenaries who wore a piece of cloth around their neck as part of their uniform. The cloth served little function save as a decorative effect, but it was a look the King liked so much that he made them a mandatory accessory for Royal gatherings. To honor the Croatian soldiers, he gave this clothing piece the name, *la cravate.*

The functional purpose of the necktie was to tie down the top of a shirt or other garment and to keep heat from escaping from the top half of the body. (Or the men were just trying to hide a hairy neck). Nonetheless, it became a fashion and a necessary accessory for someone who wanted to dress well. It complemented their wardrobe.

Here was a kind-of functional tie my grandmother used for a sore throat. She tied an egg-white soaked *mopine* (dish towel) around my neck. It hardly looked fashionable, and when it hardened to a misshapen crust of granite, making it near impossible to turn my head, I removed it and hustled away or she might summon the great "final" remedy … the evil eye, the *mal'occhio.* Sorry, I digress.

Early on, cravats and ascots were popular, but soon men's fashion became more casual as haberdashers put more emphasis on comfort, functionality, and fit. When WWII ended, the style became more liberating. The paisley or the repp-stripe were my favorites in college. I had a brief period when I wore that skinny bolo. Gad awful! And never since when Mom dressed me, did I wear a bow tie (except for with a tuxedo).

The necktie is purely a decorative accessory, and not everyone loves them. There is no good reason to wear one, particularly since it doesn't keep us warm and certainly does not add comfort. Yet many, myself included, love wearing them.

Do you see ties ever becoming almost nonexistent as did top hats and spats? I see fewer men wearing them these days. Casual is the norm.

Now that I am retired, I've taken more to turtlenecks in the winter and a casual sweater in warmer weather. But I'm an old necktie dude and love to wear them when I can. I predict that they'll be back.

The Coat Wore Me Down

During winter break during my freshman year at Providence College, I got a job delivering mail at the local Post Office. Part-time work was plentiful because, in those days, there were so many Christmas cards that there were two deliveries a day.

One blustery day, as I was leaving the house, my aunt suggested I wear my Uncle Carlo's coat: a knee-length, bulky, dark green tent-like mass with a fur lining the hood, the collar, and the inside. She had to help me put it on. Uncle was a big man. "Edward, it's very cold. This will keep you warm. Put it on. It's waterproof." Uncle Carlo was a man I admired for his heartiness, and his love of life. A former wrestler, he was powerful enough to support the coat even if the pockets were loaded with bricks. I was half his size.

I left the house wearing the coat dragging behind, hanging to my ankles. The day was a bit warmer than my aunt thought. When I reached the Post Office, I was greeted by the man who helped me load my bag. "Kind of a big coat, eh, kid?'

"Yeah. It's my uncle's. He's big. But it's fur-lined."

"Uhh ... good." He filled my bag to the brim with Christmas envelopes. Feeling the combined load of coat and mail, I got about halfway through the route when it started to snow. The snow turned to rain. The swamp green coat turned to rainwater gray. Waterproof my eye! It was absorbing the rain. As I walked, I began to feel like a fish in jelly, moving in slow motion, dragging my feet and the coat. Even the fur in the hood was damp. How could I ever finish the route under the coat?

My next stops were up a hill that grew more formidable as I eyed it.

"I'll never make it," I thought. "I'll never finish the route. I need to rest." The coat that once smelled of smoke (he was a firefighter) and cigar (well) now took on the aroma of a barnyard with a mix of straw, fertilizer, and sweat. My sweat. I was baking.

Nearby was an old wooden church. Tucking my head further down into the coat, I looked around. "Let me try the door. If it's open, I'll go in to sit just for a minute." I was in luck. The door was open. Stealthily, I rambled in, sat in a rear pew, unloaded the bag, threw off the hood, and unbuttoned the coat. The little church was empty, quiet, peaceful, warm, and dry. Perfect.

I woke sometime later. It was midafternoon. A heavy gloom overcame me. "Oh my God. I fell asleep! I gotta finish this route." The coat was no lighter, but now I was rested, and off I went. I drifted into the mailroom a little later than the others. No one said anything. Whew.

"How was the coat, Edward?" asked my smiling aunt.

"Perfect. Thanks."

Can We All Be Shmoos?

You may think I am crazy, but I feel compelled to return to the days of cartoonist Al Capp, his column *L'il Abner,* and a character you may not know; the marvelous, very quirky, and unique personality, the Shmoo.

Why? Because I want to send a message of cooperation and harmony following a contentious election in which the country has been so fragmented. A good start would be to reach across the political aisle to manage the COVID pandemic, the most pressing health crisis we have experienced in one hundred years. How could there be any difference of opinion regarding good health care for all? Bring back the central core of health care experts to educate and guide our elected leaders and our citizens. A start. A unifier.

With mitigation of the pandemic, the economy would smile like a Shmoo. Let Al Capp's quirky, unique cartoon creation be an iconic symbol.

In 1948, Capp's roving intellect introduced an armless pear-shaped personality into his daily *L'il Abner* strip. Look at this: this unusual creature loved humans, laid eggs, and bottles of Grade A milk (yes, bottles) and, in an instant, would gladly die and change itself into a sizzling steak if its hungry owner merely looked at it.

Its skin was fine leather, its eyes made perfect buttons. Shmoos multiplied faster than rabbits and tasted like any food desired. Fry it and it came out chicken. Broil it and it was a steak. The hide of the Shmoo, if cut thin, made fine leather and, if cut thick, made the best lumber. Its whiskers made splendid toothpicks.

The Character satisfied all the world's wants. You could never run out of Shmoon (plural of Shmoo) because they multiplied at an incredible rate. Anything that delighted people delighted a Shmoo who believed that the only way to happiness was to bring happiness to others. Wow, how intriguing.

Capp's readers became "Shmoo-struck." Close to one hundred of its licensed products, highly collectible today, were produced in less than a year; some of which sold five million units each, generating millions in sales in 1948 alone! They made the cover of *Time* magazine and even were air-dropped to Berliners during the Soviet blockade in 1948.

A Shmoo Savings Bond was issued by the U.S. Treasury Department in 1949!

We should capitalize on those qualities of cooperation, flexibility, kindness, benevolence, and adaptability. So how can we be Shmoo-like? Easy. Reach across the aisle, dear elected ones. Appreciate your fellow humans like the Shmoo did. Help them. Is that not what elected officials are supposed to do? It can't be that difficult.

Open the door, neighbors. Chat. Compromise. And in your discussions, be agreeable when you disagree. Incorporate the spirit of the Shmoo. Make it more than a fantasy cartoon.

The Dalai Lama said, "I remain convinced that most human conflicts can be solved through a genuine dialogue conducted with a spirit of openness and reconciliation."

I too am convinced.

CHAPTER IX

HEALTH CARE

A Leap for Alzheimer's

Diane thinks of Azheimer's disease often since her mother and two maternal aunts suffered from the problem. A few weeks ago, I appeared on GoLocal LIVE just after Dr. Steven Salloway, the Martin M. Zucker Professor of Psychiatry and Human Behavior and Professor of Neurology at Brown and Chief of Neurology and Director of the Memory and Aging Program at Butler Hospital. We had a chance to chat before our appearances. Though I knew of Dr. Salloway and his research and clinical activities (currently supported by over $3.4 million in grants), I had never met him.

It was a distinct pleasure. With all his accomplishments and recognition in the field of dementia research and treatment, he was unassuming and unpretentious. He acknowledged others: "We have the best volunteers ... the most motivated are those who have had Alzheimer's in their family. They know what it is to care for a parent or sibling."

He was a thoughtful and caring listener as I told him of Diane's family history. He had a recommendation ... that she enroll in the Butler Hospital Alzheimer Prevention Registry whose goal is to get 2,020 participants by 2020. Believing that Alzheimer's disease is the health crisis of our time, he urged people to consider participating in the program. I listened to his interview with Kate Nagle.

"So many are affected, and that number will grow as the population ages. Aging is the biggest risk factor for conditions like Alzheimer's," said Dr. Salloway. "The cost of care is greater than that for heart disease and for cancer." I was unaware. Dr. Salloway encouraged people to sign online or by phone for the 2020 prevention registry. Prevention is the key.

"We're developing treatments to remove the proteins (brain deposits in Alzheimer's) to hopefully slow down the memory loss. I think we might have the biggest impact while memory is still OK." With pride, he applauded the research being done in our State and at Brown University ... a nation-leading team.

"The investments made at Brown University, including the $100 million gift for its Brain Science Institute from Robert and Nancy Carney ... will quicken the pace of scientific discovery for diseases such as ALS and Alzheimer's."

He continued, "The earlier we go, the more effective we're going to be at either preventing or delaying Alzheimer's. We need volunteers. We need you folks out there to find out more. It's an exciting time, and I think we're in the right place to really make progress. We have developed better tests, such as a cheek swab, to see if a person is carrying one or two of the most common risk genes for Alzheimer's." Dr. Salloway's enthusiasm was infectious.

How exciting it is to see cutting-edge research in our own backyard; a perfect example of what many of us involved in health care for the citizens of our state imagine ... the impact possible with a cooperative effort.

Thank you, Dr. Steve. We applaud you and your staff. 2,020 for 2020 it will be. Let's help.

Whither Hiccupping?

Though I have been retired from the practice of medicine for some time, it is not unusual for me to receive calls for advice. I welcome them because it is reassuring to know that I might be able someone through the health care system which, at times, can be difficult. Frequent questions I am asked are: "who is a good doctor for … ; can you get me an appointment; should I get another opinion; I cannot reach my doctor, can you help, etc."

Many apologize, "I am afraid I am bothering you." My reply, "If you think you are bothering me, that's your problem. I value your confidence in me."

Last week I received a call from a dear friend who had unrelenting hiccoughs (hiccups). Because he was unable to speak, I chatted with his wife. By the time she called, he had been hiccupping for two hours. His problem jogged my memory, as I had given a lecture about hiccupping some years ago.

Hiccups (singultus) are involuntary and usually temporary spasms of the diaphragm. The distinctive hic is caused by a fast tightening of the vocal cords that follows the sudden diaphragmatic contraction. Hiccups typically start for no apparent reason and disappear after a few minutes. However, there are cases where hiccups can get out of control, lasting for days, weeks or even months. In some, the hiccups may occur up to sixty times per minute and may limit breathing.

We've all had the 'hics.' While they can be amusing when they afflict others, they can be embarrassing, painful and sometimes dangerous. There are many causes suggested for hiccups lasting more than forty-eight hours, but none have been verified. A hair in the ear, a neck tumor, gastroesophageal reflux, sore throat, some neurological disorders, excess alcohol, and some medications are among the many.

I had given a lecture on the topic some forty years ago, so I had to dig deep into my memories of home remedies before I suggested he go to the emergency room. I told his wife to try stretching his neck with head back, a hot water bottle on his upper abdomen and sucking mints which facilitate belching. A good belch sometimes works. The tried and tested breath holding may relax the diaphragm to stop the spasms.

Some remedies I had forgotten but remembered when I searched the internet were: dissolving sugar in the mouth, sticking the tongue out, pressing the thumb of one hand into the palm of the other, singing fast, laughing out loud, sticking fingers into the ears, pressing gently while rapidly sipping water, gulping ice water, and breathing into a paper bag. Oh well.

My friend's hiccups persisted, so I had his wife call the emergency squad to transport him to the hospital. He stayed the night, where after a series of tests and a fair amount of medication, his hiccupping stopped.

When I spoke with him the next morning, he was headed for a well-deserved nap. As was, I trust, his wife.

A Siren Call to Quarantine

The only time I remember anything that resembled a quarantine was confinement during WWII, when we were 'ordered' to stay in the house at the sounding of a siren. The fear of a local bombing was engendered by the 1941 attack on Pearl Harbor.

The warning meant we had to dim the lights, pull the blinds, and stay quiet. Being young and curious, I peered out the window to see a man in the darkness wearing a white hat, patrolling our neighborhood, a roaming flashlight in hand. He was a deputized air raid warden walking his beat to be sure we were following the rules. Serving as the eyes and ears of the nation's defense force, he flashed his light from house to house, window to window. I instinctively ducked. "Why do we have to stay in, Dad?"

"There may be a bomb attack. You know, there are enemy

submarines just off the Rhode Island shore where we go on summer Sundays. It'll be OK by morning." A brief shutting of the lights was nothing to resemble a quarantine but served at that time to give me a taste of incipient fear and the need to hunker down.

The practice of quarantine for diseases that can kill began during the 14th century to protect coastal cities from plague epidemics. Ships arriving in Venice from infected ports were required to sit at anchor for forty days before landing. This practice, called quarantine, was derived from the Italian words *Quaranta Giorni,* which means forty days.

In the early days of our country, little was done to prevent the importation of infectious diseases. Protections fell under local and state authorities making sporadic attempts to impose quarantines. Persistent outbreaks of yellow fever prompted Congress in 1878 to pass legislation.

In the late 19th century, outbreaks of cholera from passenger ships arriving from Europe prompted a reinterpretation of the law, giving the federal government more authority in imposing seclusion. Local authorities came to realize the benefits of federal involvement, so quarantine stations were gradually turned over to the U.S. government. Additional facilities were built, and the staff was increased. Today, federal, and local personnel respond to reports of ill travelers aboard airplanes, ships, and at land border crossings to assess the public health risk and initiate an appropriate response. There is nothing new.

Though measles, mumps, rubella, and chickenpox, are not contained in the list of quarantined illnesses, they pose a health risk to the public. We love our freedom here in America, but sometimes, for the good of all, so not to spread harm to others, that freedom must have limitations.

Listen up. Stay home. Get *all* your immunizations, children especially.

Pay attention to your health and to that of your fellow citizens. It is the one thing we can do to insure national well-being. For now, we confine with care for ourselves and our colleagues.

We are in an airborne raid. Heed the siren.

Diary of a Writer in Quarantine

For years, I have been writing a diary, and I have accumulated a cadre of notebooks with a host of things recorded, mostly about writing ... ideas, passages from great writers, books to read and reread, resources, etc. More recently, my diary has been about the coronavirus epidemic and its effect on me and my family.

Walking our peaceful neighborhood helps me generate more ideas. It is a comforting, uplifting and creative way to pass the time.

On my way, I thought of Samuel Pepys, author of the famous *Pepys' Diary*, one I read so many years ago. I remembered little of what he wrote, so I did some research (another interesting, informative way to fill time). Lo and behold, I discovered that, among many other things, he wrote of the plague in England in the 1600s. It is remarkable that what he wrote so applies to our situation today. First, a little about Pepys.

Samuel Pepys, born in London in 1633, studied at Cambridge and became a bureaucrat, rising high in government. In 1660, he began to keep a diary, recording the activities of his daily life for almost ten years. Pepys has been called the greatest diarist of all time because his frankness and the accuracy in writing of everyday British life is remarkable. His topics encompassed so much: the court, the theatre, his household, major political events, and social occurrences. I was surprised to read his writings of the plague.

The Plague, carried by rat-borne fleas struck European cities every decade or two. Pepys recorded the 1665 plague's arrival in London: 'Great fears of the sicknesses here in the City, its being said that two or three houses are already shut up.' At least 70,000 Londoners died, one in six of its inhabitants. Yet, still, on New Year's Eve, Pepys celebrated his prosperity, writing – 'to our great joy the town fills apace, and shops begin to be open again.' Optimistic, he refused to leave London's threat.

There is much to compare with our coronavirus epidemic today. *Pepys' Diary* was a monument to courage and the triumph of the human spirit. It will be so for us at some point.

In my diary, I try to capture Pepys' spirit and hope. I write of my daily walks, my readings, and my good fortune. The afternoon can be bright and cheerful. So, what if it isn't? So, what if people move over, keeping distance, screw themselves away. They say "Hello" with a smile, a cheerful sociability, notwithstanding the strained, eager, worry in their voices. An agitated desire to get outdoors can take possession of you. It's OK if it does. Make the best of difficult circumstances, for there is always someone suffering more.

I'm glad I remembered Pepys. There is a lesson to be learned from his confidence, enthusiasm, and spirit.

Try not to look at these days as gloomy. Try not to lose confidence. If you feel choked and walled in, immerse yourself in a diary. The day will improve.

Health Care Workers

I spoke with a young physician whose hospital shifts have been long and stressful, like nothing she had ever seen. "I never trained for a pandemic," she wept. "Who trains for a pandemic? So many fears ... of losing a patient, contracting the virus, of transmitting it, bringing it home to loved ones. How does anyone do it?"

"It's what I do," replied the emergency response technician during an interview I saw on PBS. "Sure, the hours are long, the fear runs deep, the pay does not match the intensity, I have no health insurance and I worry for my family. But it's what I do. And I love it. There is nothing better than helping someone who is suffering. These days, they keep on coming. It's never-ending. But it's what I do," he responded with a turn at the corner of his mouth and a heightened hesitation. I saw the fatigue hovering over these heroes.

The exhaustion is heavy, burdensome, and ever-present. The long hours and never-ending flow of sick patients; patients you cannot get to know because they cannot communicate and their families are distant, barricaded away. How frustrating. Was this man an expert on birds, hiking? Was this lady a professor, famous artist? Is this the man who I can rely upon to repair my automobile so that I, without thinking, can assume I will be safe? Can I guarantee him the same?

Our health care workers worry about doing the best they can for their patients under the worst of circumstances. Fears are palpable. An epidemic will do that ... threaten life, threaten veracity, inculcate doubt, and import waves of exhaustion.

It is an exhaustion unrelieved by coffee from the cafeteria. Eyelids close involuntarily followed by a startled awakening. Oh, how one aches for a cleansing hot shower followed by a crawl into a bed between the cold, clean sheets. I've been there during my house officer training. It can be painful.

For the first time, you realize where the pit of your stomach is, because there is the knot. It twists while you head to work. It stays for the long shift. It is eased a bit by the empathetic faces of colleagues who are tied to that same rope.

This pandemic seems biblical, like the flood or an attack of locusts. My scholar friend said, "Tristis sequella ... a morose anxiety. Morose because it never seems to end. How much suffering lies between us and the end of this epidemic? I don't know how long," he continued, "but I do know there is an end. The virus will fade; we will have a vaccine, better treatments, more hope."

This is when our workers need similar words of encouragement, a gesture, a win, a save.

"This is my job, and I love it, but I'll tell you this; this is when we need each other most."

It's what they do.

CHAPTER X
_____

TRAVEL

My First Night in Italy

Though I had read extensively and was stuffed with knowledge of Italy, it was not enough. I still wasn't quite sure what to expect the first time I traveled there. My immigrant grandparents spoke little of their country save for how difficult it was to survive. They never spoke Italian unless there was something, like a pregnancy, they did not want me to hear. Goodness, someone was pregnant! Better be sure to keep that a secret. They spoke in a unique Italian dialect, so I never had a chance to understand.

On my first day in Italy, while shopping, I heard a refined, professional answer the phone with an impressive lilting language I had never heard. *"Pronto. Si, Si. Ci vediamo."* Every syllable was articulated, every phrase a melody. He also did something the well-spoken do … he pronounced the end of every word. I was captivated, thinking, "I need to learn that language." Pride replaced ignorance and started me on my lifelong journey to learn Italian and all I could of Italy's great culture. Any apology I might have had stopped at that moment.

I began to think that my Italian origins were in some way romantic if romantic meant family, love, trust, good music, and tasty food. The more I read about Italy's culture and history, the more I needed to know. Well, what about that first night in Rome?

Our travel companion recommended his favorite restaurant, Mea Patacca across the Tiber, Trastevere. He could not have been more correct. The food, the ambiance, the company, everything was perfect. And for added value, there were strolling troubadours singing Neapolitan chestnuts, songs I heard in my grandparents' tenement. I wanted to hear my favorite, *Non ti scorda di me* ... Do not forget me.

Our friend spoke Italian. I asked him to request it. He did. The musicians knew it; had to.

The tenor was marvelous. After a bottle of wine, every tenor is spectacular in a Roman restaurant. How could he be anything but? I called across to my friend, "He was so good. I would love to give him a tip. Do you think a 'deuce' (it was years ago) is OK?"

"Don't tip him. I already did."

"What's another deuce? We're in Rome! He sang beautifully."

"I'm telling you, I tipped him. No need for anymore."

The tenor leaned over to bark in my ear, "Gimme the deuce!" I turned in a rush.

"Wait, wait. You speak English?"

"Sure, I just returned from New York where I've lived for twenty years."

My romance was not defeated, only muffled as he pointed to a small sack full of money attached to his belt. "Put the deuce here." He did say, *"Grazie"* to maintain some semblance of the romance. It wasn't necessary.

From the restaurant we wandered giddily to our hotel, gazing at history as we inched along the Roman Forum. I was not disappointed. It was Italy and I was woozy.

The Splendor of the Kentucky Derby

The Rhode Island Historical Society's upcoming event taking us back to the glory days of Narragansett Racetrack reminded me of our one and only trip to The Kentucky Derby. Watching the race on television gave us only a modest idea of what to expect.

As we approached the gates we were infused with the passion and enthusiasm of the Churchill Downs crowd; a crowd almost walking on their toes with perseverating gait in anticipation of the day. Names like Whirlaway, Seabiscuit and Man-O-War swirled in my head.

Walking along was a parade of women wearing the most fashionable hats from brassy to stylish with a mix of elegance. Flowers, feathers, bows, and ribbons of all colors conveyed their imagination and character. Men were wearing tropical colors in bold stripes, busy plaids, and bright pastels. Navy and seersucker blazers were in style.

We sat to rest, listen, and observe. I was never a betting man, but Churchill Downs, like my first time at Narragansett, whetted my appetite. I was not alone. I stood in line to bet the number four horse. It was Dad's lucky number. I won! $300! Remembering my losses – though modest – of years before at Narragansett, I returned to the stands, gave Diane the cash and sat to watch other races and the people before the Derby.

The other bet I made was in the Derby for Dad. Of course, he wanted the number four horse. I placed the bet for him. Four came out of the gate last and stayed so for the entire race. When I got home, Dad asked, "How come I never saw my horse on television?"

"Because he was dead last all the way, Dad."

"The bum." That was Dad's common refrain when sports did not go his way.

Because our hostess had means, we were invited to several elegant events. We rubbed elbows with celebrities at a tent dance with two hundred tables of ten, featuring at the same time, the bands of Lester Lanin, Salsa and Rip Rock in three different areas. The tent dance and dinner paled in comparison to the next day's brunch on a horse farm. Before the parade of horses, we toured the stables, immaculately kept.

While we stood in the picturesque portico holding mint juleps, the owners paraded several horses; all of whom had some connection with the Derby ... racers, studs, stallions, and brood mares. We were astonished. Each led by a personal handler, the splendid animals, as stylish as the ladies in their hats, pranced on the lawn. Feisty, they reared and romped to show they had spunk enough to be champions. Shining like black flowers, they were elegant and exotic with movements quick and light.

As the first Saturday of May approaches, I think fondly of our day in Kentucky. This year, with enthusiasm, I am looking forward to the swing dancers, collection items, photographs and, oh yes, the mint juleps of the Historical Society event.

CHAPTER XI

NATURE

Of Peepers and Mayflies

We are fortunate to own a lovely cabin in The Berkshires on Yokum Pond in Becket, Massachusetts. It is a great getaway, a retreat we welcome at any time of year. The seasons bring different experiences and this last weekend, we were visited by two of them: peeper frogs and mayflies.

Spring peepers, *pseudacris crucifer,* are the more famous of all the chirping frogs. They belong to a group known as chorus frogs, and a chorus it is. These delightful creatures chant with a distinctive peeping refrain that can sound a lot like tingling bells in the wind when there are many. And this weekend there was an abundance. The nights were warmer, sort of, and with windows open, we fell asleep to the music.

It's mating season, the time when the males call out to the females who are drawn to their singing suitors. After the frogs mate, the females lay their eggs underwater ... under our clean, fresh water, our pond. How interesting, even exciting, to think about the thousands of eggs dropping to the bottom of Yokum Pond. When the eggs hatch in approximately twelve days, the singing stops.

We love the sonorous sounds of the peepers; friendly visitors who lull us each evening. If we wake, they are there, serenading us under the moon and the constellations. Mixed with the peeps are other sounds … trills, hoots, quacks, and an occasional honk. If we listen carefully, we might hear a growl. It is our private symphony.

Not so much fun are the mayflies, those aquatic insects sometimes called shad or lake flies. Well … we're on a lake and it's May so the mayflies appear in swarms and mate in flight (so they say). After mating, each female lays up to eight thousand eggs in the clean, fresh water. At that point, the adults die and fall back into the water, becoming food for fish, frogs, and other aquatic life. Adult mayflies live an abbreviated time, so if you wondered, that's where they go in June, dead-in-the-water.

Though they neither attack, sting nor bite, they are annoying, nonetheless. They like the moisture in sweat, eyes, and ears and there they alight. The sheer numbers of these insects during their spring mating season are a pain. There's more.

Mayflies are attracted to light and become even more of a nuisance when they gather at night in large numbers near our doorway. It's OK. It's quite a phenomenon. It's all about nature. We love the gleeps of the peeps and their pond friends. We tolerate the mayflies.

This morning I looked at the rippling pond. There was a beaver dam in the distance, A great blue heron was posing by the edge, waiting to pierce a fish. Barn swallows were diving, flitting, catching bugs. The peepers were resting. The mayflies were spinning and twisting in the sun.

Our freshwater pond is a peaceful and pleasing delight.

The Pleasure of Hippocrates' Tree

We have a plane *(Platanus)* tree that sits overlooking the pond at our home in Becket, Massachusetts. So, what, you say. Well, it's just not any old plane tree. It is a derivative of the one under which Hippocrates taught over two thousand years ago, and ours originated from the plane tree that sits outside the Arnold Building at Brown, the former home of the Alpert Medical School's administration offices. Some years ago, my good friend, Dr. Tom DeNucci gave us the shoot.

According to legend, Hippocrates, considered the father of medicine, taught his pupils the art of medicine under its spreading boughs on the island of Kos, Greece, some 2,400 years ago.

At the 25th anniversary celebration of Brown's Medical School in 2000, attendees received an unusual party favor from medical school graduate, Dr. Pardon Kenny – a tree sapling; an offspring of the ancient plane, a descendant of the tree under which Hippocrates taught. That gift, donated so that one-day medical students might continue to learn in the shade of its storied boughs, took root. The current Kos tree, only about 500 years old, is a descendant of the original. There, it is revered and cared for just as I do mine, in Becket.

Tom gave me the shoot nestled in a bucket of mud. With care, I planted it twenty years ago, and it has taken, now standing at least twenty feet tall. My tree is in good company as saplings have been sent to other locales such as The Universities of Alabama, Mercer, Victoria, Yale, East Carolina, and Michigan. There are derivatives at The Countway Library in Boston and The National Library of Medicine in Washington.

Brown University's now mighty *Platanus* stands in a plot adjacent to the sidewalk in front of the Arnold Building on Waterman Street, where many walking by can see it, sit under it, and even think of Hippocrates and his lessons. In Becket, our *Platanus* is thriving, strong enough to have survived being bent over by crystalline ice in a recent storm. And it is now large enough for me to place a chair under it.

I walk by it often. In the silence of the pond area, I wonder, "Why do I have this tree? Am I not so lucky?" I think of Hippocrates' Oath.

While today's oath has been necessarily changed from that of the original, nonetheless it serves a purpose in recognizing the covenants of respect, integrity, education, the art of medicine, disease treatment, and prevention. One modem version, written by Louis Lasagna in 1964, ends with such phrases as "preservation of tradition and joy of healing."

I look at my tree, reaching higher each year, appreciating my good fortune to be a physician. I care for it by trimming its boughs, tying it so that it will remain ever upright, and nurturing its soil. The tree reminds me of Hippocrates and his desire to teach, the symbol of his legacy.

The Excitement of a Storm

When I was a kid, I loved the big storms. They were exciting, more than just a day out of school. Of course, now that I am older and see the climate-change-induced devastation from fires, floods, earthquakes, etc., around the world, enhanced by global warming, I have changed my mind. Why was it so thrilling back then?

I remember Hurricane Carol in 1954. Threatening, whistling winds, and snapping tree limbs were an adventure as I watched from my third-floor windows on Wealth Avenue. Yes, I will admit that I was frightened enough to scurry away every now and then. However, it was not long before I was up and hustling back from window to window, watching, not so secretly hoping, for a groaning tree to uproot.

I remember walking the neighborhood after that hurricane, fascinated by the fallen trees, stepping over downed wires, calling my friend to come out so that we could marvel at the damage. We did not equate it to another's misfortune, and I don't remember a tree collapsing a house, smashing a car, or killing someone.

I had a paper route. That afternoon, after packing my papers updating news of the storm, as I walked across Academy Avenue to deliver them, a number of eager drivers stopped, "Hey kid, can I have one of those papers? I'll give you a big tip."

I was strait-laced. "Sorry, but no. They're for my customers."

Even more exciting was to be at the Atlantic shore during a severe summer storm. My parents rented a cottage across the street from the beach, so we had a front-row seat to tempests that brewed on the horizon, promising nothing but winds and surf to pound walls and disorder beaches. Torrential rain, approaching in sheets with the rhythm of the wind, was in attack mode. Lightning streaked the darkened sky. At storm's end, we begged to go out, to walk to the rocks, a short distance away. We roamed the beach looking for treasures from the ocean's bottom or collecting a new and distinct set of shells.

The air was still swirling, raising sheets of sand that attacked our faces. When I finally got home, I was wet, shivering, and happy. Why?

It was the change. We had too many expected, bright, sunny days, and we needed that change. It was the adventure. The infrequent dreary weather of a storm did not make us sad, because, in addition to new experiences at the shore, those were the days we went to the movies in town.

A storm brought adventure, excitement, anticipation. The concern for its effect was for the adults.

Though I often looked at my father's book of the '38 Hurricane, saw its devastation, understood the loss of lives and homes, realizing it was more than a picture book, it really did not compute for a kid.

Several things have changed. The storms, now called extreme, are more frequent, seem more devastating, and certainly are more frightening.

And I am older.

What's Not to Like About a Snowstorm?

Last week, I wrote about the excitement of storms. I thought I would continue that theme by writing of snowstorms in days of old … yes, as a kid again, oblivious to the burdens of harsh weather.

Here are the lovely words of Mary Oliver's poem "Looking at a Book of … "

> *Outside, the snow floats down,*
> *it sifts through the crooked branches,*
> *it doesn't hesitate,*
> *it settles over the ground …*

It reminds me of my youthful enthusiasm as I watched the snow and sleet rapping like the tat-tat of my cap gun against the windows of our three-family home. Wind blew the snow into huge drifts high along the sidewalks and to the top steps of the first-floor porch. Eager enough though it was cold, I had a feverish desire to get out. I bundled up in my Scotch plaid red Mackinaw jacket with the big black buttons, tucked my pants into my black rubber boots and snapped them up, donned the mittens that were pinned to the jacket and, of course, slapped on the Navy toque. It was time for a snow fort and a neighborhood snowball fight.

I pushed open the door to the yard, stepped out and trudged in drifts to my thighs. The ground scrunched underfoot. The storm had slowed, leaving swirls of light snow, just enough to catch on my tongue. The cold turned on the faucet of my nose. As I reached the end of the driveway, I came upon Grandpa methodically shoveling his walk, scooping each load in a neat packet, and serving it to the top of a pile now over my head.

I snuck around to climb to the top of the mountain where Grandpa spotted me. I bounded along, dislodging clumps back to the sidewalk, some falling at his feet. With a soft scowl, he moaned, "Ed-a-wood!" and smiled.

When he went into the house, it was time to tunnel through the pile from street to sidewalk or, even better, to build a snow fort in anticipation of *the* snowball fight, the fight to the death with the losers getting a face wash with snow. We needed a formidable fort to dominate, so Dan and I packed and stacked. Behind that wall, we mounded round, firm balls of snow, ready to pelt friends, now the enemy.

Ready! Go! We winged the missiles. Under attack, we fired so fast that we depleted our cache, and all we had time to do was to scoop flat, flaky wads of snow for rapid-fire tossing. The fluffy portions flailed in the wind. No legend was born that day. I got my face washed.

The day was done. It was time to get home. Shivering and wet, bitter cold, fingers, and toes crying, face beet red, I thought of hot chocolate as in "Would you like some cocoa, Edward?" Mom always called it cocoa. Its warmth trickled in.

I loved the snow.

CHAPTER XII

WRITING

A Door Opens

How did I get to be a writer, much less now for GoLocal? Where is the connection? It is a story of an opportunity I could not refuse, especially after meeting with Josh Fenton, CEO of GoLocal. His enthusiasm is contagious.

Some years ago, I was telling my children of how lucky we were because of the bravery and courage of my immigrant grandparents who left Italy in the early 1900's for a better chance in America. They arrived with little more than a satchel and no suitable place to live. They landed on Federal Hill in Providence, connected with friends and relatives and, despite dreadful living conditions, were able to make it. They worked hard, raised families, built homes, and encouraged schooling.

My oldest son said, "I did not know that."

"My goodness," I thought. "They need to understand the story of how those immigrants made it possible for us to succeed." Realizing that I needed to document my childhood with my immigrant grandparents, I authored a story, my first of how my grandfather buried his fig tree every fall and dug it up in the spring. It was a metaphor for his courage, hope, practicality and love of the earth, the tree its symbol.

Not knowing what to do with the story, I submitted it to Bob Whitcomb, the *Providence Journal* editor. I did not hear from him for some time and then one day a call, "This is Bob Whitcomb. I think your story is charming. I am going to print it." I was speechless.

"Charming. Really?" I thought. "My grandfather's story will be told, and it will be a published." Encouraged, I authored more stories, eventually completing three books and then a monthly column in the *Providence Journal*. Here is the connection to GoLocalProv. Not long ago, I called Bob, who was now writing a Sunday column for GoLocalProv, to ask if there were an opportunity for me with GoLocalProv as I was no longer at the ProJo. I wanted to continue writing in the public domain.

"Ed," he said in his understated way, "You must write for Go Local."

And here I am, now alongside my friend and mentor and other giants ... Scott Turner, John Ghiorse, Mark Curtis, and cartoonist R.W. Alley.

GoLocal is just that, local; written for and about Rhode Islanders. I believed It would be a good fit for me because that is what I have been doing for the past ten years ... writing stories of growing up in a multi-ethnic neighborhood in Providence, Rhode Island; writing of relatives, friends, schools, teachers, travel, places and happenings. It will continue and now will also be in multimedia and video platforms.

The tag line for GoLocal: the "go to" local web experience that breaks the biggest local stories – sports, weather, news, politics, arts, entertainment – and allows users to go as deep as they wish. I love it.

I am excited about this new opportunity? Come along. Enjoy the ride with me.

I Dangle a Participle

A good sentence, no matter how long, is one that the reader can follow from beginning to end without becoming confused using bad grammar. When I write, I am constantly thinking of proper grammar, a discipline instilled in me by a remarkable teacher I had at Classical High School. More about her later.

Recently, in trying to figure where and when to place a comma, I re-read the book *Eats Shoots and Leaves* by Lynne Travis. The book has sold over a million copies since its release in 2003. No, I did not forget commas in the title. That *is* the title.

In school, we were taught the rules of grammar; rules that should never be violated. Much has changed, and there is not enough room here for me to tell you of the many changes/acceptances/breaking of rules once sacrosanct are now accepted.

For example, nowadays, it is OK to split an infinitive, use apostrophes to connote possession, join two ideas using a semicolon or end a sentence with a preposition, whereas in Ms. MacDonald's English class at Classical High School, we might be hung for doing so.

Just look at this. I was reading about a couple of grammatical techniques, one the tricolon ... a series of parallel words or phrases like football, fraternities, and fun. I think we called that alliteration. And the dangling participle, a modifier in search of a word to modify. Danglings! Horror! Spare me! My fear of days gone by has resurfaced!

Now to my story. MacDonald was a stickler for correct grammar in the spoken and written word. I shuddered when she made us present, particularly in debates. But I learned and, moreso, I learned that it was anathema to use a dangling participle. She barked, "If you use one dangling participle in a story, it's an automatic "D." If you use two, that's an "F."

For example, here is a deadly dangler that would have fired up the wrath of Ms. MacDonald: "After laying a large egg, the farmer presented his favorite chicken." It should have been, "After laying a large egg, the chicken was presented as the farmer's favorite." The farmer did not lay the egg.

For one assignment at Classical, I drafted a story which I titled, "The Tragedy."

Ms. MacDonald stood in front of the class to hand out the corrected papers. She got to mine. I waited with some anticipation for a great comment since I thought the story was so good.

"Iannuccilli wrote this story titled, "The Tragedy" and a tragedy it is. It has two, two mind you, dangling participles. I never read it once I spotted them. "F" Iannuccilli. Here's the paper." Do you think I have ever written a dangling participle since?

Grammar is the necessary bane of not just the writer, but everyone. Take care to avoid dangling modifiers or you run the risk of giving your readers an unintended reason to laugh at your work.

Don't dangle your participle.

Take Time to Write

Dad gave me an Eversharp fountain pen that fit beautifully between my fingers and, even though it leaked and stained, I loved it. My enjoyment of pens and ink was heightened when Ms. Casey taught us penmanship in the third grade. Our desks had inkwells in the top right-hand corner. We had to dip pens so significant that they had their own groove at the top of the desk.

One day Ms. Casey gave me the job of filling those wells with a narrow-funneled quart bottle of ink. The ink had a smell and color I loved, metallic with a deep purple tang and a hint of blue. Our pens required repeated dipping and the ink, having its own mind, traipsed everywhere, on papers, desk, hands, shirt and sometimes my chin. Small green blotters acted like mops. My penmanship was only promising with small letters that did not slant enough and hugged the bottom line, never quite reaching the line above. "You should slant your letters a bit more, Edward, and make them reach."

As the years went by, I stopped writing with pen and ink until one evening when I was watching an old English movie. The camera narrowed in on someone writing a letter. It was beautiful. The only things in the scene were the lustrous white paper, a quill pen, blue-black ink and two hands; fingers steadying the paper in the upper left, and the writing hand caressing the pen as if it were a baby bird. Ms. Casey would have given this careful writer an "A" for the thick, tall, looping letters and smooth strokes that loped to the top.

The beauty of that scene brought me back to the days of penmanship, paper, ink, and my love of fountain pens. I thought, "This is what we should be doing rather than e-mail and text. We should be writing to people on paper with fountain pen and ink. Even broken penmanship can be as smooth as soft summer waves. And the waves can carry the meaning."

This leads to my advice. Take pen to paper and write. Take time to write to friends and loved ones. Be yourself in your notes or letters. Transferring your thoughts with pen to paper is still the best way to communicate, because thoughts in writing come from the heart. The handwritten message is ever so much more meaningful. I love to send one. I love to receive one.

Why do I start my day at the computer looking at my e-mails? Necessity, I guess. But it will no longer be my only means of communicating over a day. My resolution is to spend some time writing with fountain pen and paper. My resolve is to fill the pen and relive my youthful pleasures.

Dad gave me his Eversharp. I now have a collection of pens that I treasure. Ms. Casey gave me the penmanship tools. They started my life-long love affair with pens, ink, and paper.

Learning is a Delicacy

I was asked to give a class on writing to sophomores at the Met School in Providence a while back. Having never given a writing class before, I was a bit puzzled.

Should I be pedantic and recite a litany of the importance of being able to write well … success comes through learning new skills, attitudes, etc. Perhaps not. Too boring. So, I decided to tell them of a learning experience in my junior high school English class of years ago.

Our teacher introduced us to poetry by reading "Casey at the Bat." I loved the poem, loved Casey, and became entranced with her recital. I was stunned when she reached the ending, "But there is no joy in Mudville – mighty Casey has struck out."

I blurted "He struck out!"

"Yes, Edward. Calm down. He struck out." I suspect that was the moment when I realized the power of the written word, my learning moment.

I read "Casey" to the class and told my story. They laughed. I reassured them that there was a sequel, "Casey's Revenge" and that the results were different.

I asked the class, "What does learning mean to you?" I was not prepared for this answer.

"Learning is a delicacy." I paused to look at the confident young lady with her smiling, wide-eyed, enthusiastic expression.

"A delicacy?" I asked.

"Yes."

"I love it," I said. "But what do you mean?"

"I just love to learn. It's like dessert."

I needed some time. I read a story from my book. The class was momentarily silent, and then they asked questions.

"Why did you write a book?"

"How many did you sell?'

"Did it make you feel good?"

"How did you remember all those things?"

"Tell us about becoming a doctor."

I said to the class, "What a treat to be in school. How incredibly lucky to learn just for the sake of learning. Savor every moment."

I reflected on those days of not listening enough, wanting to get out to do other things, sports for example.

This young lady had already realized what I learned later in life. Dessert.

Recently, I decided to re-read some of the classics that I did not appreciate as I should have in earlier years. I started with Dostoevsky's *The Brothers Karamazov*. It took one year to read. I moved on to *Moby Dick*. Another year. Then *Great Expectations*. Less time. Every page, every inch of text was worth it.

I remember the days when these assignments were a chore. Would that those years were back when I had a teacher to guide me.

To be able to learn for the sake of learning itself. To be able to enjoy the classics, history, sociology, religion, geography, and languages just because you can is a treasure, an experience like no other.

The hour sped by. I wish I had more time. I hoped they did also.

"A delicacy," she said.

Yes, indeed. We should never forget it.

"Learning is a delicacy."

Write Your Tale

Write your story; it will be your legacy.

This year, I read a book of fairy tales by Italo Calvino and heard a presentation by Greg Maguire, author of *Wicked*.

Fairy tales are entertaining; a predictable story structure, a lesson to be learned, and (usually) a happy ending. They help us to consider a range of human experiences: joy, sorrow, disappointment, fear, to name a few. They helped our ancestors make some sense of the instability of their lives as they narrated experiences of unfairness, poor treatment, and plain bad luck. They helped teach them, and us, the benefits of courage, determination, and resourcefulness.

Their stories were preserved through time by the oral tradition of storytelling. In the Italian movie, *Tree of the Wooden Clogs*, there is a scene where the *contadini*, the poor farmers, sat surrounded by family after a difficult day in the fields, and told tales. Nothing was written. No one knows where the stories arose, maybe dreams, and maybe exploits of ancestors.

Greg Maguire said, "Once we lived in the dark, but we needed light; alone, safe, in a dark cozy comfortable world."

Every life has some fairy tale. When my grandparents came to America, all they owned was in their satchels. They came to Rhode Island because they had a connection with a relative or someone from their town. They settled, found work, and worked hard.

Though life was not easy, they were living their fairy tale in the land of opportunity. They had no delusions. They knew that to survive, they needed to work. The decades following WWII galvanized many as they became absorbed into the society. My grandparents were happily at home in America and made it so for their offspring. Rhode Island was enough. They had no desire to leave their safe, new home. Their claim to America was beyond question.

I was given the chance to succeed by proud, daring people who wanted something better for their families. I write of them to never forget, to have my offspring, and others remember.

Maguire said, "Fairy tales gave light from darkness, hope from poverty." My fairy tale was living in a three-decker castle where I began to understand the importance of education.

"Light from darkness," says Maguire. What was my light? It was college and medical school. I was given a golden opportunity to take care of people and, more recently, to write of my roots. How lucky I am.

We *must* tell our story by writing, recording. Teach the young about the courage of their ancestors, their generosity, hard work and desire to survive. Help them learn about diverse cultures brought to America by so many.

Our ancestors have shaped us, moved us, made music and food for us, and taught us the value of an education and of demanding work. We must remember what people have been through to understand what we have now.

Tell your story; pay it forward. If you don't, it will be lost. And the fairy tale might end.

Purging Books

A few years ago, because our shelves were bulging, we decided to purge some books. Yes, I know, it is a painful, sometimes agonizing, decision. I was not as reluctant as Diane, but nevertheless, we undertook the task. Though we had read all the books we planned to purge, many more than once, we kept them over the years because they had become like old friends, and some we planned to read again. But it had to be done. We were out of space, and there was no way I would box the books and put them just anyplace. They deserved better.

The "to go" books were not so numerous that our task was impossible, but to do it, we had to sit by the shelves, where we picked off one book at a time. It was difficult because it was so enjoyable to rediscover what those shelves embraced.

With touching each book came the need to open, and to open meant strumming the pages, and with each strum came a stop and the time-delaying curse, re-reading. So often we found stuff between the pages; a turned-down page here, a signature there, a gift book personalized, gems tucked away such as notes, tickets, photographs, receipts, old bookmarks, a tattered spine, and a smell. Ah, the smells; musty, vanilla, dank, newspaper, toasty, glue, decaying paper and ink.

More than things to read, the books became friends in the joys and memories they rekindled.

I had a brilliant physician friend who read a paperback book a day, everywhere, when he had a moment; on the elevator, in the cafeteria, in the lounge, waiting for the next case. One day I watched him do something surprising, interesting, and painful. As he read a section, he tore if off and threw it away. "How do you do that?"

"If I didn't, they would take over my home." How very tough to do I imagined.

Books are so important because more than imparting knowledge, they not only represent moments of our lives, but also serve great purpose by improving brain function, enhancing imagination, refining vocabulary, relieving stress, affording comfort, entertaining, and bringing joy. They strengthen writing abilities. Nowadays, I can attest to the fact that they help with sleep, anytime. Books give us pleasure, taking us to foreign places, down the street or in the nearby woods.

They are storehouses for certain moments of our lives.

Well, we purged, and what do you think happened? Yes, correct. The shelves became a vacuum and we filled them, sometimes with a book we had tossed and found again in a used bookstore.

It's a useful exercise to clear one's bookshelves periodically (I think), but don't let anyone talk you into getting rid of your books if you don't want to. Keep those treasures. They will always have a place.

They are mementos to preserve until the very last.

Can you do it? Can you purge your books?

CHAPTER XIII

RAMBLINGS

The Fashion of Wearing a Vest

Not long ago, I wrote of wearing a necktie and how it was such an important part of my wardrobe when I was working. I learned from my father that good dress is a good letter of recommendation. Well, my interest was piqued a few weeks ago.

I met some friends at an event, and they were wearing vests, so nicely clad unlike so many who "dress down" in public these days. The vests were tightly woven snug tweeds, ideal accents to their sport coats. Jon looked at home and professorial. I hastened to ask, "Jon, why the vest? I like it."

"Thanks, Ed. I'm wearing it because I think it looks good and plain makes me feel respectable. And, I think more people should be dressing better, with a bit more thought." No argument there.

I was driving by one of the colleges recently and noticed several students wearing vests where once I saw only the professors wearing them … with a three-piece wool suit, of course. So, a garment we usually associate more with older, dignified gentlemen like professors, is now capturing the interest of students.

The first time I remember wearing a vest was to my junior prom in college. Dad reminded me that night to "Always leave the bottom button undone."

"Why?"

"Because if you want it to look good, that's what you do." I can find no other explanation.

Not long ago, I wrote of how my Dad rarely went out without being well-dressed, often wearing a tie, even to the cobblers. Now more incentivized, I am thinking I should be wearing a vest often, not just to accent my wardrobe, but also to feel good. I looked online and found a vintage vest store that enticed me; however, I will not buy before checking local merchants (another story).

As you might expect, there is a history to the popularity of the vest, once *de rigueur* in any gentleman's wardrobe. It dates to King Charles II of England (1630 – 1685), who introduced it to the English court as part of proper attire. The word comes from the French *"veste"* meaning jacket or sport coat, waistcoat in other locales. King Charles wanted to formalize men's wear in court. Once, no self-respecting chap would dare be caught without a waistcoat. It would be like venturing outside in underwear.

The vest can be simple wool or more elaborate silk, satin, or velvet, ideal for formal affairs. There are so many styles, colors, and fabrics. It can be worn under a sport coat or stand on its own with a long-sleeved shirt. I see more people wearing the vest casually, without a jacket. That's how the college students were wearing them.

Now, as I think more on it, the vest signals a sense of fashion that makes you feel good and less rumpled. Oh, one other thing: a vest can be slimming.

Let's jump start the trend, or at least encourage what may have started already. I will.

In This Confinement, What Do I Miss Most?

When our Governor and the Rhode Island Medical Society put out a call for doctors to help during this health care crisis, I paused a moment, just for the blink of an eye. Might I be able to do this? Might I be able to return to the hospital, the site of many an emergency/critical care encounter of my past, and help? In the next blink of an eye, I remembered my age, halt! The fleeting moment was over. Though at times I feel thirty-five, and I miss those days, no, I could never return.

That stirred me to think of what I miss during this time of confinement. I miss seeing my children and grandchildren ... their beaming faces, the lunches and dinners, and the many games they play. Texts, phone calls, face time, and Zoom (yep, I'm in) are hardly a substitute for family. A drive-by blown kiss and a wave just doesn't do it either.

I miss the coffees and lunches with friends; one of the highlights being the meetings with a group of twelve called The ROMEOs ... Retired Old Men Eating Out. We start every Tuesday at eight with an elixir or two of coffee. Tuesday, not Monday, begins our week. Save for politics, we discuss anything and everything, with a heavy accent on information and learning. The varied and fascinating backgrounds of my colleagues encourage a wide range of topics ... so interesting and stimulating that it seems as if you must get into the queue to speak, even to ask a question. But that's what makes it so appealing. It's vibrant, vital, comfortable, and never boring.

I miss a round of golf, the excitement of snapping the clubs out of the trunk, walking to the first tee to the tapping of irons, setting the terms of the match, teeing up the ball, taking a few practice swings and *bam!* Off we go. A walk in the park. Birds cheering us on, clouds moving us along and the fuzzy, tired, slightly achy feeling at the finish.

I miss going to the movies, a night out to dine, concerts, the barber ... oh yes, the barber.

I miss leafing through the pages at bookstores and libraries with their lingering aromas of familiarity.

I've learned spatial intelligence and sweeping detours, so I miss the friendly hug. I miss shaking hands. I know. Things change, of necessity these days. Wallace Stegner writes, "How simple and memorable a good day can be when expectation is low." The days are good because, with lower expectations, I see daylight. I hear the start of the car's engine, the clanging of restaurant dishes, the snap, snap of the clippers, the circumlocutions of a ROMEO, the tap of the conductor's baton, the smell of movie popcorn.

Now, the gloomy gravity comes with what I miss most. I miss having the choice to do these things.

Lessons From the Hawk and the Dove

When you're confined to quarters, one form of exercise is to make house rounds from window to window, hoping for a trace of excitement, something more than the circumventing walkers, whizzing bikers, and bounding dogs.

Outside our breakfast room window is our bird feeder and a birdbath, sources of enjoyment and solace. The yard is replete with cavorting cardinals, gorgeous goldfinches, capering chickadees, working woodpeckers, delightful doves, and trolling squirrels. On a day last week, a surprise hit us.

As we were gazing with coffees in hand, a rufous-colored, medium-sized Cooper's hawk burst from the sky above and pounced on an unsuspecting victim just below us. We have seen these hawks often, usually at a distance in the tree in the next yard, but never so close.

Because she had spread her wings to hide the catch, we were not immediately aware of what it was. As she moved warily, she lifted her wing and, there, we saw a lifeless dove, killed with the drop. The hawk jockeyed to fix the prey in her talons. As she lifted her wing, another hawk, a male, came swooping in with a darting gesture toward the possessor. He speared the prey but was unable to hold it. The captor covered and repositioned her captive and flew off, dove in claws.

We were as silent as a held breath when a parent tells us not to move. Then we chatted about the wonder of nature we had just witnessed, reflecting upon whether there was a lesson in what we saw, a metaphor of today's pandemic?

Captor, captive, survivor, loser. Who wins during this pandemic? Who loses? What have we learned? Have we been as efficient as that hawk? Or as complacent as the dove? Who would guess, by the way, she sauntered about pecking treats from the ground and not paying attention just before, that death would befall this beautiful creature?

We, unlike the dove, must pay attention, not be complacent, follow directions, watch, and be wary. We, like the hawk, must be ready to pounce on whatever it takes to overcome the virus. Who wins? Well, for now the first attacker, coronavirus. Like the hawk, this virus came in fast and low, like a phantom appearing out of thin air.

The powerlessness of being unprepared can be staggering. We cannot let it happen again. We cannot be the dove, vanquished with little fight. We must be as efficient as the hawk. Efficiency? It's listening to experts and following directions. It's wandering from window to window for now. It's changing our health care system so that all are better prepared for later.

I am in the house and, though passive while following the recommendations of experts, I am more like a hawk, ready to pounce on what will keep me safe. Unlike that dove, I'm paying attention. In the days to come, we must be strong and efficient.

Emerge stronger. Be the hawk.

Once Masks Were Fun

My neighbor stopped at a distance, of course, to say hello. He was wearing a mask that he made from a striped sock. "I like the look."

Muffled words leaked through the cotton, "Mum ... muph, King Tut."

Everywhere I go, albeit not far these days, I see people wearing masks. Good for them! They are necessary in this pandemic because they help to keep us from spreading or contracting the virus. The last time I saw so many masks was in the hospital. I wore one to enter the room of a patient in barrier or to go to the operating room where everybody wore them. That was, and this is, serious business, but in my youth, masks were mostly fun.

At Halloween, I wore one as part of my costume to become my favorite masked characters: Superman, The Lone Ranger, or a 'bad guy' with a bandana. I once wore a gas mask and played 'Army' in the local hills, mimicking the soldiers in the WWII movies. Today, some of the most iconic images from movies wear masks, like Hannibal Lecter in *The Silence of the Lambs,* or Darth Vader.

Whereas those masks were entertainment, todays are not. For centuries, masks have been used for numerous reasons, e. g. to ward off evil spirits (sound familiar?), for protection, like the welder's mask, gas masks, and shields on gladiators' helmets. And now, the critical masks for our health care workers.

So why the masks? A mask will do a decent job of reminding you not to touch your face, something that can increase your chances of becoming infected with the coronavirus. In some studies, it has been noted that people touch their faces up to twenty times per hour. A mask may protect you from an infected person's sneeze or cough droplets. The droplets can be caught or directed downwards.

A sizable portion of those infected with coronavirus don't show symptoms. Under those circumstances, a mask may protect you.

A few studies have suggested that widespread use of face masks by the public may have reduced transmission in outbreaks of influenza and SARS which, like Covid-19, are respiratory diseases.

Put the mask on with clean hands, replace it as soon as it becomes damp, remove it from behind without touching the front, wash your hands afterward, and dispose of the mask properly. Do not reuse a mask made for a single use.

An important note: The use of masks by healthy people may create a false sense of security, leading some to neglect essential measures such as handwashing, disinfecting surfaces, avoiding people who are sick, and keeping a distance from others. A mask does not eliminate the need for these precautions.

Face masks are like King Tut's gold. Treat them as such. Wear them. Listen to experts. Pandemics can threaten your life. They should threaten your conscience also.

It's no joke. It's not kids play. It's serious. We should listen to the hoofbeat of fear.

A Man Who Is Making a Difference

Recently, I have been writing about people and organizations that make a difference by giving back to humankind. One name kept coming up, Bob Aldrich. "If you want to meet someone who gives back, talk to Bob." I did.

Bob Aldrich, an unassuming, understated man with a kind, serious demeanor, comfortably discussed his passions. What I thought might take an hour or so took two. That is how interesting his story is. "When I retired from Raytheon as director of operations in 2004, I thought, I'm not quitting. There's more I want to do." A friend told him of a project in northern Cambodia in the village of the Siem Reap Province.

Sixteen years ago, Bob ventured forth, met the director of the hospital (a R.I. native by the way) who told him of a major issue in the community with water borne infectious diseases, particularly in children; cholera and E. coli the more prominent. Not only did these diseases keep kids out of school with diarrhea and dehydration, but they were also, on occasion, deadly.

Bob researched and learned of a simple water purification system using biosand filters that would help, particularly in homes. The filters would be shipped to the village, assembled, and put to quick use. Bob helped install the first thirty.

Gravity fed; these simple filters are household units that produce clean water directly from contaminated sources. Polluted water is poured in the top, filtered through sand and gravel layers and, within minutes, clean drinking water pours from the spout. 95+% of protozoa and bacteria are filtered out. The water looks and tastes good; a decided advantage over well water where high iron content has an offensive taste and color. One filter can produce enough clean water for a typical rural family for many years.

Today, the filters are made in Siem Reap from locally available materials by a staff of fifteen. They assemble 2000 filters per year, and now have over 25,000 in homes and schools serving a population of 150,000. The incidence of debilitating diarrhea has dropped remarkably. Kids not only can go to school, but they can also stay in school.

Nowadays, Water for Cambodia is a vibrant, non-government, non-profit organization (www.waterforcambodia.org). They also operate a water testing lab that monitors filter performance. This holistic approach is helping to break the cycle of disease and poverty.

Bob Aldrich has made, and continues to make, a difference in a third world country, contributing toward its stability and growth.

After over sixteen years of work in a place where Bob and his wife Beth travel every year for two weeks, he remains enthusiastic. "I love the country. I love the people … I have a good understanding of their culture. The project is close to my heart."

That's not all. Energetic, enthusiastic, and committed, he still had an instinctive and restless urge to do more. Locally, he serves on Bristol's Comprehensive Planning Committee, and is a strong advocate and worker for open spaces, transportation, efficient use of space, and saving Bristol's harbor.

Yep. Talk to Bob.

Does Zoom Work for Me?

When I was a kid, if I was zooming, it was on my Rocket Royal Monarch Bike. Zoom meant speed, wind in my face, passing houses in a blur. Or it meant sound, *the* sound, the one made by clipping a playing card to the wheel frame with a clothespin, making sure it was in a place so the flying spokes would hit the card and snap in cadence to explode the rhythmic effect of an engine, like a motorcycle that zoomed. Vroom … Zoom … Vroom.

Today, to Zoom is quite different. It is a video conferencing service used to virtually meet with others, either by video or audio only, or both. It is the phenomenon catalyzed by the threat of a menacing virus that has kept us confined. No longer are meetings over lunch or coffee or at a round table.

I hated conference calls. I wanted to see body language, the shuffling of papers, the twitchy leg, the spilled coffee, and the broken pencil when someone was anxious, or fibbing, or whatever. It took a while for me to get used to Zoom.

Now, I Zoom weekly with our Italian group, hosted by a retired Brown professor, and I have grown to enjoy it. Sure, it will never replace our meeting in the Italian restaurant over pasta and wine, but this works … for now.

During the initial meetings, I fumbled. It seemed I was watching Hollywood Squares, the old TV show. When anyone wished to speak or made a noise like banging the table, their square lit up. Then, my neurosis jumped in. I experienced the, "I feel like I'm on television," effect. Oh! I don't want them to see me with a collarless shirt. I jockeyed my screen so that I wouldn't look too old or too pale or too anything. What's behind me? Grandchildren pictures, of course.

Then, I was asked to mute because of a barking dog (not mine), a wailing child (not mine), and a cell phone (mine). Really.

It did not take long for me to get over myself and into the learning, listening, speaking Italian. Forget appearances. We were in the classroom and, at home. And learning.

I hit the Zoom height three weeks ago when we had a reunion of my 1957 Classical High School class. There were so many participants that we needed two sessions. It was successful because it allowed graduates from all over the country to attend without having to travel. Though our friendships were less touchy, they were still palpable.

So much in our lives have shut down: schools, bookstores, libraries, museums, restaurants, movie houses, and the theater. Sure, Zoom has enabled successful social distancing and has fostered digital learning, but it has taken me a bit to get used to being away from the warmth of the in-person gathering.

Nonetheless, it is the one way you can stay home and stay sane while still in communication with family and friends. Does Zoom work for me? It works, for now.

What Color is Your Parachute?

I enjoy interviewing students who are applying to medical school. Of late, I have offered them a grounding interview so they can anticipate, understand, and comfortably answer any question. I instruct them on how to position themselves as a worthy, qualified, desirable applicants; how to separate themselves from a competent crowd. The interview also helps me if I am asked to write a letter of recommendation.

I had not heard the question until the day my grandson was interviewed for Providence College (he was accepted). His evaluator was a former trustee, professor, community leader, banking official and savvy interrogator who asked me to sit in. I listened with some apprehension, but I quickly relaxed as I saw how well Andrew was handling the questions. Until this one, dropped in at the end: "Andrew, what color is your parachute?"

"Uhhh, I don't have a parachute."

"That's OK. Don't worry about it." 'You did very well."

I wondered where the question originated. I too would have been stumped. It stemmed from a popular self-help book, *What Color Is Your Parachute?* by Richard Nelson Bolles and is the world's most popular, self-help, job-hunting guide, with more than ten million copies sold. Among many things, it is a practical manual that provides essential tips for writing resumes and cover letters, networking effectively, and interviewing with confidence.

I liked the question so I thought I would use it in my interview of medical school applicants with the intention of improving their chances of getting accepted, helping them prepare, enhance their competitiveness, and seeing how they might react to a curve ball query. The answers were interesting, amusing (one quite humorous), and informative.

– My parachute is black. – Why black? – Because I always see the glass half full. I'm a pessimist. – I am surprised. Your responses to my questions reflect confidence. Where did that answer arise? – My mother. She's a worry-wort.

– Well, don't let that come across in your medical school interview. Change that attitude. – OK, good advice, Dr. I. He was accepted.

This answer from an entertaining young man was more amusing. I reviewed his resume before the interview. It was impressive ... good grades, a good test score, wonderful letters, top-notch extracurricular activities, including research. But it was not one that stood out as so many of the well-qualified applicants I had seen hit the same marks.

I always look for something different. And I was pleasantly surprised.

He answered with an amused, easy confidence. – Teal! My parachute is teal.

– Teal? Why teal? – Well, maybe because I am an Improv actor and have been doing it in a company for two years.

– Improv? Why is that not on your resume? – I didn't think it was that important.

– Young man, it is what sets you apart from your competition. Be sure to include it.

I had never met an Improv actor. Teal. I loved it.

Yes, he too was accepted.

I Flunk the Draft Test

I was an intern at Rhode Island Hospital in the summer of 1965, undertaking my responsibilities with enthusiasm and thoughts of little else but medicine. One day, I received a letter from the local draft board stating that I had to report to the nearby examining station.

I called. "I'm a doctor in training. I think I'm exempt."

With a heavy groan, a gruff reaction followed, "Git down here." Bang went the phone. The next morning, I took a bus to the Fields Point Station some blocks away.

"Yes?" I heard as I walked through the door. I showed up wearing my hospital whites, hoping to be dismissed as soon as they saw me. At the desk was a sergeant with his head down. Before hearing my plea, he barked, "Over there! Get in the line!" I tried to talk to another soldier. "Sir, I am a doctor in training."

"There!" he pointed. With a deep breath, I stood in line with a collection of wide-eyed, barely breathing young men. We entered a large room rimmed with a white line on the floor. "Everything off!" I had heard from friends about what induction physicals were like.

"Everything?" came a chorus in unison.

"You heard me. Toes on the line!" Someone, maybe a doctor, came by to check us ... throat, neck, heart, lungs, other things. I asked if this was an induction physical. No answer.

"Get dressed. Go to the next room. Take a seat! Fill out your information, then start answering the questions." We sat at long tables with test papers in front of us. At the top of the page, next to where we had to print our names, was the question, "Number of years of schooling?" I added them up; college and medical school piled on the others totaled twenty. I looked to either side at my mates.

"Look ahead! Eyes on the test!" There were pictures of machine parts. Not recognizing anything, I was unable to answer a single question of what they were or how one matched another – carburetor, spark plugs, ignition wires and tools, lots of tools. I was stumped. The boys on either side seemed to be doing well, marking answers with a marching step. Pictures familiar to them were unfamiliar to me. I sat staring at the page with a blank look when the sergeant stopped by.

"You did all these years of school!"

'Yes, Sir."

"Well, how come you're not answering?"

"Because I am a doctor and never saw anything like this."

"You should not be here. You should never have been called. Now get out, Doctor."

"Yes, Sir."

As I boarded the bus to return to the hospital, a known world for me, I was disturbed with the futility of my morning, though relieved that I would be staying home. I knew where I was going as the bus tugged me back to the hospital. I thought of those boys who answered the questions so well. An unfamiliar world was ahead for them.

∞

ABOUT THE AUTHOR

Ed Iannuccilli, M.D., a retired gastroenterologist, has had extensive experience in academics, management, governance and entrepreneurial endeavors. Former Chairman of the Board at Rhode Island Hospital and a former member of the Lifespan Board, he is a Clinical Professor Emeritus at The Warren Alpert Medical School at Brown University.

He was the founder of CME Consultants, a national physician and professional education company.

Dr. Iannuccilli is a graduate of Providence College and Albany Medical College. He is a published author of medical articles and of stories of his childhood. Dr. Iannuccilli has been on numerous boards and was honored as the distinguished alumnus of Albany Medical College in 1991.

Currently a weekly columnist for GoLocalProv, he is the author of four books:

> *Growing up Italian: Grandfather's Fig Tree and Other Stories*
> *What Ever Happened to Sunday Dinner and Other Stories*
> *My Story Continues: From Neighborhood to Junior High School*
> *Growing Up Italian: Collected Stories (E-Book)*

Made in the USA
Middletown, DE
02 April 2023